Drug Therapy and Obsessive-Compulsive Disorder

Psychiatric Disorders
Drugs and Psychology for the Mind and Body

Psychiatric Disorders: Drugs and Psychology for the Mind and Body

Drug Therapy and Obsessive-Compulsive Disorder

BY SHIRLEY BRINKERHOFF

MASON CREST PUBLISHERS

PHILADELPHIA

Mason Crest Publishers Inc.
370 Reed Road
Broomall, Pennsylvania 19008
(866) MCP-BOOK (toll free)

First printing
1 2 3 4 5 6 7 8 9 10

Brinkerhoff, Shirley.
Drug therapy and obsessive-compulsive disorder / by Shirley Brinkerhoff.
p. cm.—(Psychiatric disorders: drugs and psychology for the mind and body)
Summary: Examines the obsessive-compulsive disorder, its symptoms and manifestations, how it can be controlled and treated, and what it is like to live with obsessive-compulsive disorder. Includes bibliographical references and index.
1. Obsessive-compulsive disorder—Juvenile literature. 2. Obsessive-compulsive disorder—Chemotherapy—Juvenile literature. [1. Obsessive-compulsive disorder.] I. Title. II. Series.
RC533.B745 2004
616.85'227061—dc21
2003002385

ISBN 1-59084-569-2
ISBN 1-59084-559-5 (series)

Design by Lori Holland.
Composition by Bytheway Publishing Services, Binghamton, New York.
Cover design by Benjamin Stewart.
Printed and bound in the Hashemite Kingdom of Jordan.

This book is meant to educate and should not be used as an alternative to appropriate medical care. Its creators have made every effort to ensure that the information presented is accurate—but it is not intended to substitute for the help and services of trained professionals.

Picture Credits:
Artville: pp. 14, 16, 21, 39, 47, 81, 90, 93, 94, 98, 102, 106, 121. Autumn Libal: p. 53. Benjamin Stewart: p. 68. Comstock: pp. 41, 74, 78. Corbis: p. 76. Digivision: p. 56. Image Source: pp. 62, 64, 97. PhotoAlto: pp. 12, 34, 44, 89, 100, 117. PhotoDisc: pp. 24, 25, 29, 31, 36, 48, 57, 58, 59, 66, 77, 79, 83, 84, 86, 104, 109, 112, 114, 122. Quigmans: p. 118. Rubberball: pp. 71, 80. Stockbyte: pp. 10, 20, 23, 108. The individuals in these images are models, and the images are for illustrative purposes only.

CONTENTS

INTRODUCTION

by Mary Ann Johnson

Teenagers have reason to be interested in psychiatric disorders and their treatment. Friends, family members, and even teens themselves may experience one of these disorders. Using scenarios adolescents will understand, this series explains various psychiatric disorders and the drugs that treat them.

Diagnosis and treatment of psychiatric disorders in children between six and eighteen years old are well studied and documented in the scientific journals. In 1998, Roberts and colleagues identified and reviewed fifty-two research studies that attempted to identify the overall prevalence of child and adolescent psychiatric disorders. Estimates of prevalence in this review ranged from one percent to nearly 51 percent. Various other studies have reported similar findings. Needless to say, many children and adolescents are suffering from psychiatric disorders and are in need of treatment.

Many children have more than one psychiatric disorder, which complicates their diagnoses and treatments plan. Psychiatric disorders often occur together. For instance, a person with a sleep disorder may also be depressed; a teenager with attention-deficit/hyperactivity disorder (ADHD) may also have a substance-use disorder. In psychiatry, we call this comorbidity. Much research addressing this issue has led to improved diagnosis and treatment.

The most common child and adolescent psychiatric disorders are anxiety disorders, depressive disorders, and ADHD. Sleep disorders, sexual disorders, eating disorders, substance-abuse disorders, and psychotic disorders are also quite common. This series has volumes that address each of these disorders.

Major depressive disorders have been the most commonly diagnosed mood disorders for children and adolescents. Researchers don't agree as to how common mania and bipolar disorder are in children. Some experts believe that manic episodes in children and adolescents are underdiagnosed. Many times, a mood disturbance may co-occur with another psychiatric disorder. For instance, children with ADHD may also be depressed. ADHD is just one psychiatric disorder that is a major health concern for children, adolescents, and adults. Studies of ADHD have reported prevalence rates among children that range from two to 12 percent.

Failure to understand or seek treatment for psychiatric disorders pust children and young adults at risk of developing substance-use disorders. For example, recent research indicates that those with ADHD who were treated with medication were 85 percent less likely to develop a substance-use disorder. Results like these emphasize the importance of timely diagnosis and treatment.

Early diagnosis and treatment may prevent these children from developing further psychological problems. Books like those in this series provide important information, a vital first step toward increased awareness of psychological disorders; knowledge and understanding can shed light on even the most difficult subject. These books should never, however, be viewed as a substitute for professional consultation. Psychiatric testing and an evaluation by a licensed professional are recommended to determine the needs of the child or adolescent and to establish an appropriate treatment plan.

FOREWORD

by Donald Esherick

We live in a society filled with technology—from computers surfing the Internet to automobiles operating on gas and batteries. In the midst of this advanced society, diseases, illnesses, and medical conditions are treated and often cured with the administration of drugs, many of which were unknown thirty years ago. In the United States, we are fortunate to have an agency, the Food and Drug Administration (FDA), which monitors the development of new drugs and then determines whether the new drugs are safe and effective for use in human beings.

When a new drug is developed, a pharmaceutical company usually intends that drug to treat a single disease or family of diseases. The FDA reviews the company's research to determine if the drug is safe for use in the population at large and if it effectively treats the targeted illnesses. When the FDA finds that the drug is safe and effective, it approves the drug for treating that specific disease or condition. This is called the labeled indication.

During the routine use of the drug, the pharmaceutical company and physicians often observe that a drug treats other medical conditions besides what is indicated in the labeling. While the labeling will not include the treatment of the particular condition, a physician can still prescribe the drug to a patient with this disease. This is known as an unlabeled or off-label indication. This series contains information about both the labeled and off-label indications of psychiatric drugs.

I have reviewed the books in this series from the perspective of the pharmaceutical industry and the FDA, specifically focusing on the labeled indications, uses, and known side effects of these drugs. Further information can be found on the FDA's Web page (www.FDA.gov).

Obsessive-compulsive disorders may first become noticeable in a school setting.

1 | Defining the Disorder

September, sophomore year

Today was my first day of classes at the high school. Mom and Dad made a big deal of it at dinnertime, like being in tenth grade was something to celebrate. They kept talking about how high school could open up whole new "worlds" for me and asking if I was going out for track again ("think about all those records you broke back in seventh grade, honey") or if I thought I might join the Spanish Club ("you know how they take those wonderful trips to Mexico every year, dear!").

It would have made me really mad if I couldn't see how hard they're trying. Even though they won't come right out and say it, you can see that they keep hoping I'll be like the old Amanda again some day—the Amanda who used to wake up excited about running; the Amanda who loved to travel more than anything in the world.

What they don't know is that the old Amanda is gone.

If this situation weren't so weird, it'd almost be funny. I mean, think of me trying to run track while I'm counting steps

and making sure I land on the right foot. Or picture me travel-
ing to Mexico with the Spanish Club, sharing a room with
three other girls. You tell me which three girls in my class
could ever understand why I have to get up at 4:30 in the
morning just to spend an hour and a half in the shower.
They'd all be off sightseeing, and I'd still be doing my stuff in
the shower . . .

In one way, it'd be easier if I could just explain it all to my
parents. If I could ever just look them in the eye and say,
"Look, I can't do any of those things anymore. You see, there
just isn't time." Then they'd ask what I meant, and I'd tell
them—the way I have a million times in my head—but I
know they'd never understand.

Sometimes, I picture myself explaining it all to a psychia-
trist, who could maybe make my family understand.

A person with obsessive-compulsive disorder may have to per-
form certain rituals each time she eats.

"It was that first week of 8th grade when it started," I'd say, "the week the teachers decided I should be in advanced placement math. Everybody thought it was so cool that I was that good at math, even my best friend Emma—correction: make that my former best friend Emma—who used to get jealous that I was always on the honor roll and she only made it now and then.

"But something happened to me when I started that math class. It was like I felt all this pressure to make sure I got every single problem perfect, like I couldn't let anybody down by making a mistake. So I had to check my work. Not like I used to, when the teacher always said, 'Okay, everybody check over your papers before you hand them in,' and we all glanced at our problems for two whole seconds before we passed them forward.

"This was a totally different kind of checking. One day, I had to rework every single problem. I remember Mrs. Wilson, my math teacher, finally saying, 'Come on, Amanda. My next class is going to start in just a few minutes.'

"I looked up, and everybody from my class had left already. But I felt nervous in the pit of my stomach, as though I'd better check all over again. Mrs. Wilson wouldn't let me, though. She just smiled and took my paper, then shooed me into the hall. 'Go on now, Amanda. I'm sure you did just fine.'

"After that, things started getting weird. At first it was just math. I'd do the problems, check them, then have to check them again. If I didn't, I'd feel like something really bad was going to happen, but I didn't know what.

"Then I started having to count my steps. Like, 387 steps to the bus stop, and if I missed one or lost count, I had to go home and walk it all over again until I was sure I got it right. There had to be 387, no more, no less. At school, I started having to count steps from each classroom to my locker. They had to come out to exactly the right number, and I had to start and end each walk on the same foot or—guess what?—I had to *walk it all over again. That's when I started getting sent to the office for being late to classes. That's also why I had to drop out of track. Ever try to run the quarter mile and make sure you take the exact number of steps you did the last time?*

"At first, I worried a lot about why I was counting steps, but then I just stopped thinking about it, maybe because the problem of checking my homework just kept getting worse and worse and was taking all my time and attention. After a couple of weeks, I was reworking my math problems eight, nine, even ten times. My parents kept asking me what I was doing. Every night, they'd say, 'Amanda, what's wrong? Why is your homework taking you so long these days?' When I told them I just had to check my work to make sure it was done right, they were proud of me at first, proud that I'd be so careful and all. But after a while, they started to worry. 'Amanda, it's okay, really. We're sure it's right. You're such a good stu-

Some people with OCD may feel compelled to count or chant a word for each step they climb.

dent, Honey, your homework is almost always right.' They just didn't get it. I appreciated what they were trying to do, but reassurance had nothing to do with that weird, anxious feeling inside that said I had to keep checking.

"Finally, my parents got irritated with the whole situation. They saw how tired I was and started forcing me to go bed by 11:00. One night, I knew I wasn't finished. I waited till I was sure they must be asleep, then I got up and worked my math problems all over again. It still didn't feel right, so I did them another time. I think I did that paper ten times, maybe eleven, before I felt like I could quit.

"After a couple months, math wasn't the only thing I had to check and recheck. If I read a short story or a biography for literature class, I always had to read them again, over and over, in case I missed something, even though I didn't know what. Pretty soon, there wasn't time in my life for anything but homework.

"At first, Emma kept calling me, wanting to talk for an hour at a time like we used to, but I had to tell her I had too much homework. Then she'd get all hurt and say, 'Listen, Amanda—I know how much homework you have. We're in exactly the same classes, remember? So why don't you just tell the truth and admit you don't want to talk to me anymore?'

"But I didn't know what to say. How do you explain something you can't understand yourself? Finally, she got mad and quit talking to me at all. After a while, I saw her hanging around with Trish and Lisa.

"Things kept getting worse at home, too. There was no way I could keep up with my chores, and my little sister, Nikki, got all upset because she said I wasn't doing my share of the work, which led to a lot of arguments. But I was too busy to care much what everybody else said. And I still am— but not because I want to be. Because I have to be.

"That's what I wish someone could explain for me, not just to Mom and Dad, but to Emma, who never even speaks to

me anymore, just rolls her eyes whenever she and her new crowd see me in the hall. And I wish someone could explain to my teachers, too. Some of them seem like they might even be nice—if I ever had time to get my homework finished. But once they see my homework is always late, that I never finish my tests on time, they'll think I'm just one more kid who couldn't care less about school, who just wants to mess around and waste time."

That's what I'd tell someone—if I dared. But there's no use wishing. Nobody will ever understand what's going on inside my head. If they found out, they'd stamp "Crazy!" on my forehead and send me away so fast it'd make my head spin.

One individual with OCD followed a complicated invisible maze as he went around his house each morning. If someone stepped in his way before he completed his ritualized route, he felt he had to start over at the beginning.

WHAT IS OBSESSIVE-COMPULSIVE DISORDER?

It is estimated that there are as many as six million people in the United States who suffer from the same problem that Amanda has, an anxiety disorder known as obsessive-compulsive disorder (OCD).

In modern society, the words *obsessive* and *compulsive* are often used in connection with activities such as gambling or substance abuse. While it is true that many people abuse drugs or gamble with a sense of compulsion and in a way that seems obsessive, these activities usually provide some pleasure, at least in the beginning. True obsessive-compulsive disorder, however, is a mental disorder with very specific features, including compulsions, which are not at all pleasurable. According to the *Diagnostic and Statistical Manual of Mental Disorders* (DSM-IV, the most recent classification of mental disorders by the American Psychiatric Association), features of OCD include:

- recurrent obsessions or compulsions that are severe enough to take up more than one hour a day or that cause marked distress.
- the person's recognition that the obsessions or compulsions are excessive or unreasonable.

A patient is not diagnosed with OCD if their disturbance is due to the effects of an abused drug, a medication, or to a general medical condition.

> **GLOSSARY**
>
> **obsessive:** Having to do with thoughts that are excessive, often to an unreasonable degree.
>
> **compulsive:** Cravings that are intense and often repeated.

SYMPTOMS OF OBSESSIVE-COMPULSIVE DISORDER

The symptoms of OCD differ widely from person to person, but they most often include checking, washing, and recurring thoughts (called ruminations). Some OCD patients

have obsessions; others have compulsions. In some patients, both are present.

Obsessions

Obsessions are ideas people cannot force out of their minds. These ideas may range in content from repetitive thoughts of a certain number, a group of words, or a pornographic image, to an intense fear that the sufferer has killed another person without realizing it. The four most typical topics of obsessions are dirt, harm, sex, and religion.

Compulsions

Compulsions include actions and *rituals* that seem senseless, such as washing one's hands for several hours each day or stopping between every word one reads to count to fifty.

GLOSSARY

rituals: Repetitive activities, often distorted exaggerations of some daily routine.

OCD IN HISTORY

This disease has been recognized for centuries, although not necessarily by the name we use today. Samuel Johnson (1709–1784), who was a poet, biographer, playwright, and scholar, and was considered one of the greatest men of his time, exhibited some of the common symptoms of OCD. His friend Miss Frances Reynolds and his biographer, James Boswell, described Johnson's unusual rituals, including his habit of spinning, twisting, and then actually jumping over door thresholds. Johnson also counted his steps to determine which foot should be used to enter the doorway. Other passages tell how Johnson never stepped on the cracks in paving stones and how he touched every post along the road when walking with friends. If he missed touching a post he returned to touch it, leaving his friends waiting until he had done so.

Samuel Johnson.

In 1894, the physician-in-chief at Johns Hopkins Hospital, Sir William Osler, described a thirteen-year-old girl he had examined who had

> occasional twitching of the muscles of her face and neck noticeable in the sudden elevation of the eyebrows. . . . A short time after the onset of the twitchings . . . she began to have all sorts of queer notions and practices. . . . Before getting into bed at night, she lifts each foot and taps nine times on the edge of the bed. After brushing her teeth she has to count to one hundred. . . . On reaching the door, she knocks three times on the edge of the window nearby, and three times on the door before unlocking it. She will not under any circumstances button her shoes. In drinking water she will take a mouthful, then put the tumbler

A person with OCD may have lengthy bathing rituals. . .

. . . or demanding exercise routines.

down, turn it once or twice and repeat this act every time she drinks. Before putting on clean underclothes she has to count so many numbers that there is a great difficulty in getting her to make the change except under the strongest threats from her mother.

Another historical figure with OCD, this one from the twentieth century, was the wealthy businessman Howard Hughes. Hughes feared germs from the time he was a child, a fear that eventually grew into a life spent behind sealed doors and windows, in darkened rooms where aides brought him papers or meals using special tissue pads that kept them from actually touching anything Hughes might touch. Hughes had rituals connected with eating, grooming, and dressing that took up many hours of his day. As with many sufferers of OCD, his rituals eventually became so overwhelming that he was incapable of keeping up with them. In the end, Hughes was dirty and unkempt, his hair was matted, and his nails grew so long they curled in upon themselves. He dressed in only a pair of undershorts or went nude.

Dr. Rapoport, in *The Boy Who Wouldn't Stop Washing*, comments that her own patients—many of whom are neither rich or brilliant or glamorous—fight many of these same battles, not just every day, but in some cases, every hour. "Their hands and arms are red or even bleeding from continual washing. Their desks and drawers are uselessly arranged, the rules controlling this behavior based on some sterile, abstract sense of order." She refers to the "crazy" thoughts that dominate her patients' lives, adding that, although most psychiatrists don't use the word *crazy*, it is important to recognize that this is how the patients themselves think of their OCD behavior. "Since they are so sane in every other way," Rapoport writes, "you must agree with

---

Most Common Obsessions in OCD

- repeated thoughts about contamination, as in being contaminated by shaking hands
- repeated doubts, such as wondering if one has hurt another person; wondering if one locked the door
- the need to have things in a specific order and experiencing intense distress when confronted with disorder
- aggressive/horrific impulses to do such things as hurt a loved one or say obscenities in church
- sexual imagery, such as pornographic images

A person with OCD may feel the need to check and recheck his school work. No matter how smart he may be, he will take far longer than other students to complete his assignments.

and understand how upset they are by how crazy it all is." This is in keeping with the fact that OCD patients recognize their symptoms to be *ego-dystonic.*

In his book *The New Psychiatry*, Jack M. Gorman, M.D., tells the story of a man named Ronald who was hospitalized because of his compulsions:

> He cannot sit down in a chair until he carries out a rigidly prescribed series of actions. He must first brush the seat of the chair, then the back, then the seat again. Each brushing must include 26 strokes to the left and 26 to the right. Then the chair must be turned to the right four times, then left four times, and turned completely around eight times. There is more, and the entire compulsion takes about 30 minutes. If a single mistake is made, Ronald must start all over again.

GLOSSARY

ego-dystonic:
Alien thoughts, not the type of thoughts one would usually have, and not within one's control, though still the product of one's own mind.

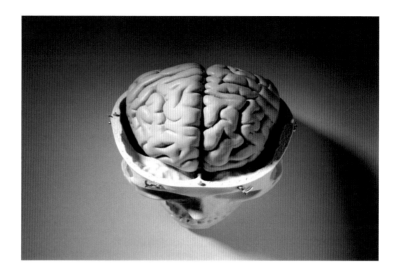

A model of the brain's frontal lobe.

Gorman goes on to describe Ronald's other rituals, which are so demanding and time-consuming that Ronald, like other patients who suffer from severe OCD, sometimes decides not to get out of bed in order to avoid them. "Ronald cannot give a reason for all of this and will tell you he wishes he could stop. But he has given up trying to resist for many years."

WHERE DOES OCD COME FROM?

Theories about the causes of OCD fall into four main categories.

Brain Abnormality

Researchers have speculated that OCD may be rooted in abnormalities of the ***basal ganglia***, a region deep within the brain. In comparison with subjects who do not have OCD, those with obsessive-compulsive disorder have been shown by **PET scans** to burn energy more rapidly in areas connecting the **frontal lobe** and the basal ganglia. The more severe the OCD, the more rapidly the energy is burned. Some researchers feel that this increased **metabolism** may actually contribute to the unusual way in which patients with OCD respond to and process information.

Autoimmune Neurological Disorders

A newer theory linking childhood OCD and strep throat was first reported in 1997 by psychiatrists Susan Swedo, Judith Rapoport, and their colleagues at the National Institute of Mental Health (NIMH). In the late 1980s, the link between OCD and Sydenham's chorea (known earlier as Saint Vitus' dance and a frequent childhood disease before the discovery of antibiotics) was being studied. Sydenham's

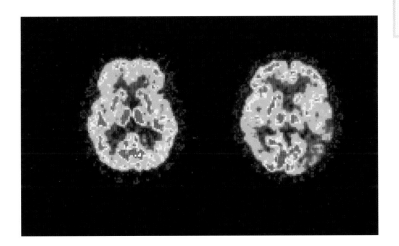

Magnetic resonance imaging (MRI) provides detailed brain images. Some researchers suspect that OCD may be caused by abnormalities deep inside the brain. One day MRIs may help scientists detect these abnormalities.

GLOSSARY

PET scans:
Positron-emission tomography. A brain-imaging technique.

frontal lobe: The part of the cerebrum (the upper, and largest, section of the brain) covered by the frontal bone.

metabolism: The chemical changes in the body through which energy is provided to the cells.

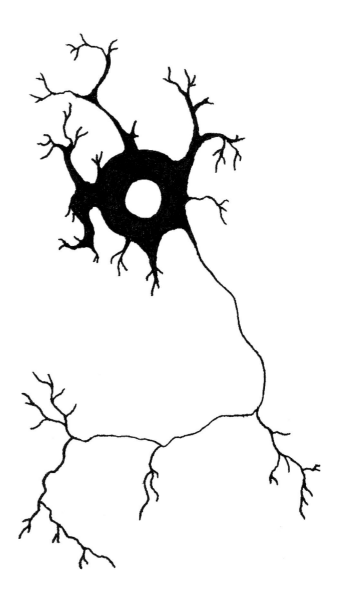

A nerve cell.

chorea, an ***autoimmune disease*** with neurological symptoms ranging from clumsiness to unrestrained flailing of
the arms and ***delirium***, results in the production of antibodies that attack the brain. Brain-imaging studies done on
patients with this disease show inflamed, bulging basal
ganglias. Group A beta hemolytic streptococcal infections
(known to most of us simply as "strep throat") also produce
antibodies that not only attack streptococci cells but normal
cells as well.

Because Sydenham's chorea is often characterized by
obsessions and compulsions similar to those of OCD, researchers began asking if childhood OCD could be, like
Sydenham's, caused by autoimmune damage to the basal
ganglia, possibly as a result of strep throat. After much research, it is now considered likely that up to 25 percent of
childhood OCD may originate with strep throat and the resulting autoimmune damage to the basal ganglia.

Chemical Imbalance

Nerve cells in the brain transmit messages to one another by means of chemical substances called neurotransmitters, such as serotonin. (For a more detailed explanation
of how the brain works, see chapter three.) People with
OCD may lack the amount of serotonin needed for effective

GLOSSARY

**autoimmune dis-
ease:** An illness
that initiates or re-
sults from the pro-
duction of auto-
antibodies
(antibodies that
act against the
body's own mole-
cules and tissues),
sometimes with
damage to normal
components of
the body.

delirium: A disor-
der characterized
by impairments in
consciousness,
attention, and
changes in
thought pattern.

Most Common Compulsions in OCD

- washing/cleaning
- counting
- checking
- requesting/demanding assurances
- repeating actions
- ordering (placing objects in definite, orderly patterns)

GLOSSARY

bipolar: *A psychological disorder characterized by extreme highs and lows.*

phobias: *Fears brought on by the presence or anticipation of a specific object or situation.*

nerve cell communication. Other neurotransmitters that may also be involved are norepinephrine (which is related to stress) and dopamine (which is related to thought and movement disorders).

Heredity

Studies of twins and other first-degree relatives of people with OCD show a higher incidence of the disorder among closely related family members. This leads researchers to conclude that the disorder may be inherited. Close relatives of those with OCD also show a higher than usual occurrence of major depression, **bipolar** illness, panic attacks, severe **phobias**, and neurological problems.

Although researchers have not proven a biological basis for all cases of OCD, doctors such as Jack M. Gorman point out that OCD symptoms do not seem to be linked to life stresses or to negative experiences in childhood. They are,

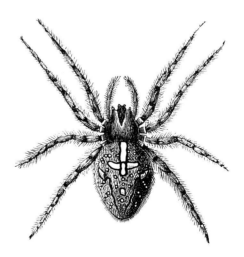

Relatives of people with OCD are apt to have other psychiatric disorders—such as intense phobias. A person with one form of phobia, for example, would be intensely afraid of spiders.

Researchers study twins in order to better understand the role genetics plays in OCD.

GLOSSARY

trauma: *A distorted psychic or behavioral state resulting from mental or emotional stress or physical injury.*

epileptic seizure: *A disruption of motor ability as a result of a neurologic disorder called epilepsy.*

aneurysm: *An abnormal blood-filled blister of a blood vessel or artery.*

however, sometimes known to develop in a previously healthy person after traumatic brain injury or brain infection.

Dr. Rapoport tells of two children with no previous signs of OCD, who then suddenly developed OCD symptoms after *trauma*. The first case involved an eleven-year-old named Steven who had his first *epileptic seizure* a week after his birthday. Though his epilepsy was controlled through medication, his life began to be dominated by the number four, to the point that he was no longer able to manage school or to have any fun.

In the second case, an eight-year-old named Jacob was rushed to the hospital after playing football with his older brothers. He had collapsed in a coma from a bleeding cerebral *aneurysm*, but a four-hour surgery repaired the damage. Jacob recovered with amazing speed, and yet when he woke up, he had to touch everything seven times. Dr. Rapoport reports, "he swallowed seven times and asked for everything in sevens. Multiples of seven and, worst of all, the *time* it took to do everything by sevens, filled his day in the hospital. . . . He could only go back to school when the touching-counting compulsion was stopped by treatment with Anafranil."

These cases, along with findings of the brain-imaging studies and the genetic components, lead some scientists to theorize that OCD is indeed a biological disorder.

THE DOUBTING DISEASE

One of the most fascinating aspects of OCD is the way in which some people become unable to know that they know certain things. There are many accounts on record of people like Jerry, who locked his door at bedtime and then found himself unable to go to bed until he had checked it as many as forty to a hundred times each night. Jerry found this compulsion to check and recheck his door lock maddening. Even though he could see for himself that the door was locked, he had to keep checking to relieve the feelings of anxiety that something bad would happen to him or his family if he didn't check.

In French, obsessive-compulsive disorder is known as *foie pourquoi* and *folie de doute*, or "the doubting disease." For most people, seeing that the door is locked is enough. They then "know" that information. People with obsessive-compulsive disorder, however, cannot "know" certain things no matter how many times they check, or look at the evidence, or think through the situation. This inability to know certain things is not a defect in intelligence or memory, and those with OCD have no more difficulty knowing most things than the average person. In a very selective way, OCD seems to target certain kinds of knowledge, and only those are doubted; hence the common symptoms of checking

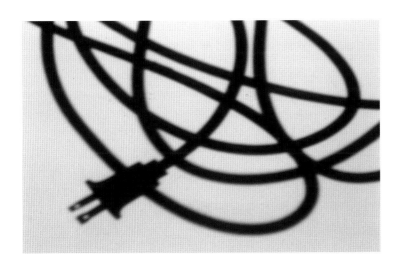

A person with OCD may check and recheck to be sure she has unplugged an electrical appliance. No matter how many times she looks, her doubts will make her look yet again.

door locks and light switches. People with OCD usually function well in other areas of their lives. Many professional people have obsessive-compulsive disorder and have learned how to cope with their symptoms and perform successfully in their careers.

As Dr. Judith L. Rapoport explains in *The Boy Who Couldn't Stop Washing*, "A much more complex cognitive or perceptual process (than intelligence or memory) has gone wrong. . . . Something in the mind—in the brain—goes wrong." Dr. Rapoport poses the question: "Is some mental filter working well for the rest of us that isn't working for them?"

The problem centers on knowing how to know. Catherine became convinced that she was responsible for someone's death. Her case was so severe that she was hospitalized, where she spent hours sobbing and begging for reassurance from the doctors and nurses. When they questioned her as to why she believed this, the story was always the same. "I *could* be the cause of someone's death. I *could* have been driving too close to someone—tailgating—and made them angry, and they could have had a heart attack and I would never even know. How can I know I didn't hurt someone that way?" When reminded that she was a kind and considerate person and could never have been responsible for someone's death, Catherine became even more agitated. "That's what everyone says," she answered. "And it's no help at all!"

Other people with obsessive-compulsive disorder may feel compelled to turn a light switch on and off, on and off, over and over. This act "brings immediate information," says Dr. Rapoport, "yet it doesn't *get through*." They can't get the feeling of *knowing* the light is off. People with OCD in this situation are usually well aware that something has gone haywire in their thinking processes. They are not looking for reassurance; they are desperately trying to regain their ability to know.

Some children with OCD ask the same questions over and over. Giving them the answers will not ultimately help them, because it is not necessarily information they are seeking but the feeling that now they know that information. One patient asked repeatedly what color the leaves were and what color the sky was, but answers did not help. She had lost her ability to know green and blue.

At some point, however, repeated door-checking and light-switching do work, though only temporarily. This adds to the patient's confusion, because they learn that if they keep checking, eventually they can know what they're seeking, at least until their ability to know cuts out again. By the same token, compulsive hand-washers reach a temporary *plateau* of feeling clean enough. Then the compulsion returns, and they are compelled to begin washing again.

Although obsessive-compulsive disorder has many frightening and seemingly bizarre symptoms, it is important for people with the disorder not to keep their condition secret. OCD does not mean a person is mentally ill or crazy; instead, it means there is a part of the brain that is not functioning normally. Very often, this malfunction can be treated successfully with drug therapy.

> **GLOSSARY**
>
> *plateau:* A stable, level period.

OCD may hinder a person's academic performance.

2 | History of the Drugs

*A*pril, *sophomore year*

I got into trouble again this morning for taking so long in the bathroom. My sister, Nikki, was hammering on the door, yelling about how did I expect her to get ready for school when I was always hogging the shower.

She didn't know it, but her interrupting me just made it worse. It meant I had to start all over again: Rub the top of my head ten times, then put one drop of shampoo where I rubbed. Then rub the front left side ten times, then put one drop of shampoo there. Then the front right side, then the back left, then the back right. There are about a hundred other steps for each shower, but I don't have time to write them all out. Then I have to do it again without the shampoo, to rinse it. I was hurrying as fast as I could, and I almost made it.

But then Mom got into the act—I guess Nikki went and told her I was hogging the shower. Mom started banging on

OCD may cause a person to check and recheck a mathematical problem. No matter how many times he checks it, he will wonder if he did something wrong and have to check it all over again.

the bathroom door and telling me I had to have some consideration for my sister, and that messed up the whole pattern. I had to start all over for the third time.

I don't know how much longer I can keep this up. It took me until 3:00 A.M. to finish my math last night, and I had to set the alarm for 5:00 A.M. so I could shower. Every four or five days now, more steps get added to the pattern. It's getting so complicated I can hardly remember it all, but if I don't, I know something bad will happen. There's no other way but to keep doing this. But how will I remember it all if it keeps getting more and more involved? And then I'll have to get up earlier, and I can hardly keep my eyes open in classes as it is.

The strangest part about checking my homework over and over is that, in some part of my head, I really think I worked those problems right the first time last night. I usually do. But even when I've checked them and checked them over and over, it's like with some little part of my brain I know they must be right, but something inside me keeps pushing me and pushing me to check again. It makes me think that if I just check one more time, then I'll know for sure. But sometimes it takes me a dozen or more times now to get to where I feel I really know it. How crazy is that? But I can't stop; I don't dare, because something will happen if I do. It's like I'll explode or something. I don't even know how to explain it to myself anymore. I just know I have to keep doing it all.

The shower routine is exactly the same kind of feeling. It has nothing to do with getting clean. It's just this feeling that I have to do things in this certain order, and if I don't, something will happen. It's enough to drive you nuts.

I just read what I wrote, and I had to laugh. I'm obviously nuts already! I have to get back to homework now. I don't really even have time to write in this journal anymore, but if I don't, I feel like I'll fall apart. This is the closest I can ever come to telling anybody what's really going on.

Obsessive-Compulsive Spectrum Disorders

Other disorders that are similar to obsessive-compulsive disorder (in that they include obsessive thoughts and/or compulsive behaviors) include:

- body dysmorphic disorder
  (Patient is preoccupied with an imaginary defect in his appearance, most often in his face.)
- trichotillomania
  (The individual repeatedly pulls out her own hair, most often that of the scalp but also eyelashes, eyebrows, and other body hair.)
- eating disorders
  (Anorexia nervosa, a failure to maintain body weight at or above a "minimally normal" level, and bulimia nervosa, a pattern of binge eating and the consequent use of "compensatory behaviors" such as fasting, purging, or exercising to avoid gaining weight.)

Just a few decades ago, little real help was available for people in Amanda's situation. But now, Amanda and others like her who suffer from OCD have several psychiatric drugs available to help combat this disease. These drugs include clomipramine hydrochloride, fluoxetine hydrochloride, fluvoxamine maleate, sertraline hydrochloride, paroxetine hydrochloride, and citalopram hydrobromide; information on each follows.

THE TRICYCLIC ANTIDEPRESSANT (TCA): CLOMIPRAMINE (ANAFRANIL)

One of the first psychiatric drugs to show promise in OCD treatment was clomipramine, marketed under the name Anafranil, first approved for use in the United States in

Scientists discover psychiatric drugs by studying the effects of various chemicals on brain cells.

1990. Several years prior to approval, the National Institute of Mental Health began an extensive study of OCD in adolescents throughout the United States. Researchers were especially interested in finding out whether Anafranil would help adolescents with OCD as much as it was helping adult sufferers in other countries where the drug was legally available. The drug manufacturer, CIBA-Geigy Pharmaceutical, helped researchers obtain Anafranil for testing purposes, and a special license was given for research use here in the United States.

Prior to 1990, clomipramine had been used for more than thirty years outside the United States as an antidepressant, and its antiobsessional qualities were well known.

Brand Names vs. Generic Names

Talking about psychiatric drugs can be confusing, because every drug has at least two names: its "generic name" and the "brand name" that the pharmaceutical company uses to market the drug. Generic names come from the drugs' chemical structures, while brand names are used by drug companies in order to inspire public recognition and loyalty for their products.

Here are the brand names and generic names for some common psychiatric drugs used to treat obsessive-compulsive disorders:

Anafranil®	clomipramine hydrochloride
Celexa®	citalopram
Luvox®	fluvoxamine
Paxil®	paroxetine
Prozac®	fluoxetine hydrochloride
Xanax®	alprazolam
Zoloft®	sertraline hydrochloride

Years of research lie behind each psychiatric medication on the market today.

Although officially known as a tricyclic antidepressant, there is some discussion as to whether clomipramine should be classed as an antidepressant or antiobsessive, but it remains an important and effective drug in the treatment of OCD.

THE SELECTIVE SEROTONIN REUPTAKE INHIBITORS (SSRIs)

Fluoxetine (Prozac)

Fluoxetine was first found to be effective in treating OCD in the mid-1980s, in the course of two major studies conducted in the United States. *Side effects* were significantly lower in patients on fluoxetine than in patients on clomipramine, although treatment effectiveness was equivalent.

Drug Approval

Before a drug can be marketed in the United States, it must be officially approved by the Food and Drug Administration (FDA). Today's FDA is the primary consumer protection agency in the United States. Operating under the authority given it by the government, and guided by laws established throughout the twentieth century, the FDA has established a rigorous drug approval process that verifies the safety, effectiveness, and accuracy of labeling for any drug marketed in the United States.

While the United States has the FDA for the approval and regulation of drugs and medical devices, Canada has a similar organization called the Therapeutic Product Directorate (TPD). The TPD is a division of Health Canada, the Canadian government department of health. The TPD regulates drugs, medical devices, disinfectants, and sanitizers with disinfectant claims. Some of the things that the TPD monitors are quality, effectiveness, and safety. Just as the FDA must approve new drugs in the United States, the TPD must approve new drugs in Canada before those drugs can enter the market.

Fluvoxamine (Luvox)

Developed in Europe as an antidepressant, fluvoxamine appears to be equally effective as clomipramine and fluoxetine in the treatment of OCD. Small-scale trials were conducted to determine fluvoxamine's antiobsessional effects in the late 1980s. In the 1990s, two important studies were conducted in the United States that gave convincing evidence of the drug's efficacy in treating OCD.

Sertraline (Zoloft)

Sertraline has been shown to be effective in treating OCD, without the side effects of clomipramine. A drug trial in the late 1990s, which specifically studied children and adolescents with OCD, and another study done to compare its effectiveness with clomipramine, yielded positive results as to sertraline's effectiveness. It appears to be equal to the other SSRIs.

Paroxetine (Paxil)

Paroxetine has been demonstrated to be effective in the treatment of OCD in several studies, including two twelve-week controlled studies of adult outpatients who all had moderate to severe OCD. A twelve-week study in Italy (1997) compared the effectiveness of paroxetine, fluvoxamine, and citalopram, and no significant differences were found.

Citalopram (Celexa)

Citalopram is the newest SSRI to be released in North America and is at present used for treatment of depression. However, it has a long history in Europe of use for anxiety conditions and is expected to be proven as a useful treatment of OCD. Systematic trials in OCD treatment are now under way.

Obsessive-compulsive disorder can restrict a person's academic and social life.

3 | How Does the Drug Work?

*S*eptember, junior year

Okay, today something bad happened, then something good happened. So maybe the good will cancel out the bad, and I'll be able to hold my ground.

The bad thing was that, at about one o'clock this morning, when I was rechecking my trig homework, I had to get up and lock my bedroom door. It was just that feeling—you know, that something was wrong, or something was coming at me that would be bad—the same kind of thing that makes me keep checking my homework. No one else would understand why this matters, because if they were trying to decide whether or not to lock their bedroom door, they'd just think it through and then make a decision. But this feeling is different from making a decision. It's like something in my mind that isn't me is giving me orders—orders I don't dare disobey.

(I sure hope nobody ever finds this journal. Can you imagine what people would think if they read this?)

Anyway, I tried to fight the feeling for a while (I'm always scared that new crazy stuff is going to pop up inside my head like this, because that's how the shower routine and the checking started), then I gave in. "Fine, then!" I said, "I'll lock it already, all right?"

And I thought that was the end of it. Which shows you how much I know! About three minutes later, I get this feeling like I'm not sure if the door is locked. I look up from my desk and I can see *the lock, but I still feel like I need to get up and check it.*

At first I refused. I was absolutely determined not to give in. But I don't know why I even try, because obviously I have about as much self-control as a bagel. So I checked the lock. And then I had to check it eighteen *more times! I can't believe it's happening again, with something new. Sometimes I wish so much that I had somebody else's body, or at least their mind. Or that I was just a whole different person. I can't imagine living for the rest of my life with a brain that does such weird things. Actually, I don't even have a life. I just check things; that's all I do. (If you don't count taking showers.) So that was the bad thing that happened, and I woke up so depressed I could hardly stand it.*

Then today this really good thing happened—amazingly good! I was registering for the classes I have to take this year, and the guidance counselor said I'd better fit driver's ed into my schedule somewhere because that was a really important thing to learn. I don't know why, but for some reason I just figured I wouldn't be able to do driver's ed. Maybe because that's what normal people do, and I always feel as though everybody must be able to just look at me and see how un- normal I am! But apparently that isn't what the guidance counselor saw. So I signed up! And you'll never guess what else. The absolute hottest guy in the world is in my class, and he actually sits right in front of me. I'm hoping that maybe

Some individuals with OCD may be compelled to perform certain ritual actions at various times during the day for specific periods of time. As a result, they may be obsessed with timing themselves as they go through their days.

he'll be part of my driving group. I don't know his name yet, but maybe tomorrow—!

Anyway, I never really thought much about having my license before, not seriously. I guess that's because most of the time I'm too busy checking. And showering, and checking some more. But maybe things will change if I get out more, like the other kids. You know, drive to the mall, stuff like that. Lately, I've been thinking about how things were before all this craziness started inside my head. I think I used to be pretty normal. I mean, I had friends and I ran track and I really liked to go shopping with Emma. I remember Mom used to drop us off at the mall on Saturday morning, and we'd stay there till late afternoon, trying on stuff and having fun. Back then I used to just do my homework once, period. And then forget about it. It seems like a dream when I look back on it now.

But like I said, maybe driving will help change things. . . .

Keeping a journal promotes self-awareness. It can be an important first step toward healing.

When Either Psychiatric Medicines or Psychotherapy May Work

When a patient exhibits:

- depression that does not include suicidal thoughts, loss of function, or inability to eat or sleep
- panic disorder
- generalized anxiety disorder
- social phobia
- bulimia

Adapted from *The New Psychiatry*, by Jack M. Gorman, M.D.

November

Well, the driving's going okay. I'm pretty good at it, actually. But I may as well forget about Dylan (that's the guy that sits in front of me in driver's ed class.) At first, he was really friendly. He even came and ate lunch with me in the cafeteria one day, but I should have known it was too good to last. Coach Sanders, the teacher, kept giving us worksheets to do in class. (I don't think he likes to teach very much, and the worksheets keep us busy.) We're allowed to talk quietly after we hand in our worksheet for the day, and Dylan kept turning around to talk to me that first week of class. But I was always checking, and rechecking, and then re-rechecking my answers. Long after everybody else was done, I was still working. He finally started talking to Anna, who sits in front of him, and I saw them eating lunch together the other day. Now when he even remembers I'm there in the seat behind him, he looks at me like I'm slow. Like maybe my mind's not up to par, and

he's wondering why I'm in a class with all the "normal" people. I should have known he was too good to be true.

OCD can seem overwhelming to those who experience its symptoms, but there is hope. Many people who struggle with OCD, as Amanda does, have found help by using drugs developed in the last few decades, drugs that can markedly decrease—and sometimes totally wipe out—the symptoms of OCD.

When these patients experience the positive results of their medication, they don't always realize what is going on inside their heads, where the medicine affects brain neurotransmitter levels, such as the serotonin and noradrenaline systems. In order to really comprehend how such drugs operate, it is important to first understand a little about how the brain works.

BRAIN FUNCTION

The sheer complexity of the human brain is amazing. Inside are millions and millions of neurons—specialized brain cells that are capable of passing on messages to other neurons. There are so many neurons in our brains that if all the neurons with their axons from a single human brain were stretched out end to end, it would go to the moon and back.

The brain does not operate alone. It is part of the central nervous system (CNS), which also includes the spinal cord. Between the brain and the central nervous system, each individual has billions of neurons, both sensory and motor. Our five senses—sight, hearing, smell, touch, and taste—feed information from the outside world to the brain by way of the sensory neurons. Motor neurons respond to this information by making the muscles of our bodies move.

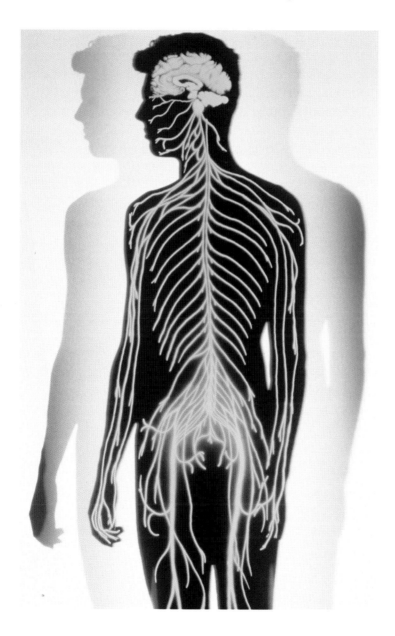

The nervous system is made up of the brain, the spinal cord, and billions of neurons.

How does this vast communication system work in real life? Let's say that Jimmy, who is too young to understand the dangers of fire, is roasting marshmallows by threading them onto a long stick, then holding that stick over an open campfire. In a hurry to get to the good part (eating a nicely browned, gooey marshmallow), Jimmy inches closer and closer to the fire so his stick can reach the hottest part of the flames. Unfortunately, he gets a bit *too* close. When a flame flares up suddenly, it makes unexpected contact with Jimmy's little finger, stimulating a nerve cell there.

In a flash, the nerve cell in Jimmy's finger conducts a message about the situation along its axons to the spinal cord. There, information is relayed to other neurons, which send information back to Jimmy's hand, telling it to move. *Fast.*

However, that's not the end of the message relay going on just then in Jimmy's body. If Jimmy doesn't learn from this experience that fire can hurt, his little finger could face the same kind of danger again in the future. So the information that fire is hot—and that he should keep his hand away

---

When Psychiatric Medicines May Be Needed

When a patient exhibits:

- suicidal thoughts
- presence of hallucinations or delusions
- decrease in ability to function (includes inability to sleep, eat, work, care for children, perform personal hygiene)
- self-destructive behavior
- uncontrollable compulsions (constant washing or checking)

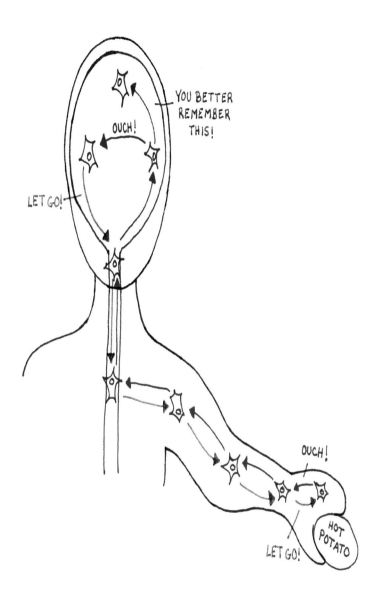

When we pick up a hot potato, our neurons carry messages to our brain and back. The brain also learns to avoid this experience in the future!

from it—is relayed to yet other neurons, and this important information is stored in Jimmy's memory.

Neurons are irreplaceable. While other areas of the body, such as skin or hair, replace dead cells with new cells of the same type, the brain is different. It has always been thought that once the brain or the spinal cord is injured, those injuries are permanent, because once neurons die, the body does not make new neurons. Today, however, some scientists are questioning this.

How do messages, or neural impulses, travel through the body to the spine or brain? Much of the answer lies in the structure of the neuron itself. In one area of each neuron the cell body sends out dendrites, projections that look like tiny twigs. In another area of the neuron the cell body

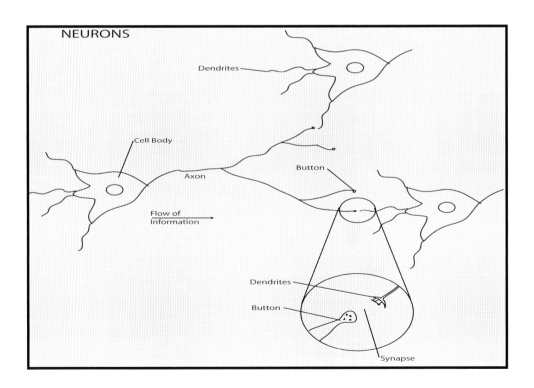

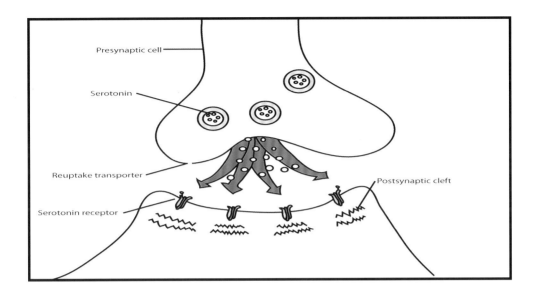

extends a long, thin *filament* called an axon. At the end of the axon are several terminal buttons. The terminal buttons lie on the dendrites of another neuron, so that each neuron functions as a link in the communication chain. The chain does not run in just one direction, however. Because each neuron is in contact with many other neurons, the CNS is like a vast mesh or web of interconnected groups of neurons. It's amazing to consider the communication connections and interconnections possible between these millions of neurons, with their cell bodies, axons, and dendrites.

Brain cells communicate by sending electrical signals from neuron to neuron. Although axons and dendrites do not actually touch other neurons, they are very close together. Between cells is a tiny space called a synapse, and through this space nerve impulses travel, jumping the gap in much the same way an electrical current would. When a message is to be transferred, a neuron "fires," and its terminal buttons release chemicals called neurotransmitters (biochemical substances such as norepinephrine and dopa-

GLOSSARY

filament: A long, thin series of cells connected to each other.

Scientists study brain activity at the most basic, microscopic level.

mine), which make jumping the synapse possible. When an electrical signal comes to the end of one neuron the cell fires, secreting the proper neurotransmitter into the synapse. This chemical messenger then crosses from the presynaptic neuron (the brain cell sending the message) to the post-synaptic neuron (the brain cell receiving the message), where it binds itself to the appropriate chemical receptor and influences the behavior of this second neuron. Neuro-transmitters can influence the behavior of the postsynaptic neuron by either transmitting the message or by inhibiting the passage of the message.

When the neurotransmitter binds to the receptors, other processes are set in motion in the postsynaptic brain cell, either exciting it to keep sending the message along or in-hibiting it to stop the transmission of the message. After the impulse is passed from one neuron to another, the neuro-

Our brains are as complicated as any computer's circuitry.

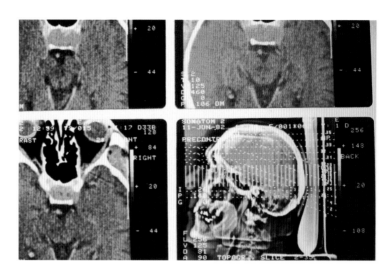

Imaging techniques allow researchers to look inside the brain as they search for the answers to psychiatric disorders.

transmitter falls off the receptor and back into the synapse. There it either goes back into the presynaptic neuron (a kind of neuron recycling), gets broken down by ***enzymes*** and discarded to spinal fluid surrounding the brain, or reattaches itself to the receptor, thus strengthening the original signal traveling from the presynaptic neuron.

There are at least one hundred billion synapses in the brain. Researchers presently know of about thirty different neurotransmitters, but new ones are being discovered all the time; there may be hundreds. And many neurons respond to more than one neurotransmitter.

It is in this complex environment of the brain where psychiatric drugs operate, usually by influencing neurotransmitters. The operations of these drugs are more complex than this, but their main function is to make the postsynaptic neuron either more or less likely to fire.

Different classes of drugs operate in different ways. The drugs commonly used to treat obsessive-compulsive disorder include SSRIs and TCAs. As we discussed in chapter two, the first two medications to show significant impact on OCD were clomipramine (a TCA, often known as Anafranil) and fluvoxamine (an SSRI, often known as Luvox). In recent years, several more drugs in the SSRI category have been made available for treatment of OCD. These include fluoxetine (Prozac), sertraline (Zoloft), and paroxetine (Paxil).

Anafranil remains the only TCA to show real effectiveness in treating symptoms of OCD. Anafranil strongly affects the metabolism of serotonin in the brain and actu-

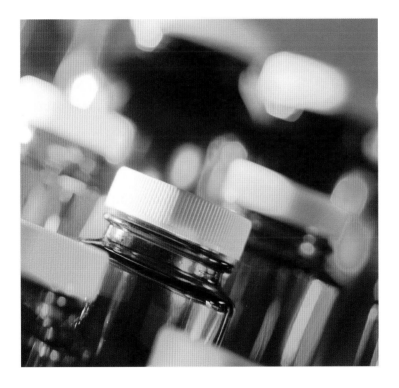

Different kinds of drugs affect the brain in different ways.

ally increases the amount of serotonin available to brain receptors.

Serotonin is vital for many functions and has been related to depression, anger, and impulsivity. The symptoms of obsessive-compulsive disorder are also part of the brain functions to which serotonin has been related. The exact way in which it works, however, remains a mystery; Anafranil may influence other brain chemicals that are affected by serotonin. The SSRI drugs listed above also increase the amount of serotonin available to brain receptors, but usually have fewer side effects than Anafranil.

In his book *The New Psychiatry,* Dr. Jack M. Gorman stresses the importance of a patient's knowing whether or not the prescribed medication is working. "The one advantage of medication over other forms of psychiatric treatment is that an effect is usually discernible in a matter of weeks; no one should ever continue to take medication unless it is clear there is a benefit." In order to assess this, he encourages patients to realize that psychiatric drugs *cannot*:

- improve one's basic personality;
- give job success or a better marriage;
- make one smarter, more athletic, or a better parent.

Instead, their effect—usually quite concrete—is to relieve and often eliminate specific symptoms. For those with OCD, these specific symptoms include obsessions and compulsions.

Drugs cannot only work or fail, they can also work partially, in which case they would reduce target symptoms but not eliminate them. If this happens, the doctor and patient face the decision of whether or not to raise the dose, add a second drug to augment the first, change drugs, or turn to ***psychotherapy*** without drugs. ***Behavior therapy*** alone sometimes provides partial relief for people with OCD, but

GLOSSARY

psychotherapy: *A treatment method in which a person who wants to resolve problems or to seek personal growth enters into formal, ongoing conversations with a person trained in psychology.*

behavior therapy: *A treatment method that focuses on what can be observed and manipulated, leading to a change in behavior.*

medication is the most effective treatment. The two therapies are often used in combination or in sequence.

In *The Boy Who Couldn't Stop Washing,* Dr. Judith Rapoport tells the incredible story of Laura, who preferred to allow herself to be sent to a school for children with mental retardation rather than to tell people about the compulsions she was experiencing. Laura was in her twenties when she consulted Dr. Rapoport. She had married but was seeking help in regard to the almost nonexistent relationship between herself and her husband. Her compulsions to check things and to wash had to be finished before she could have time with her husband. Add to this her compulsion to hoard things and the time she had left to do anything else was meager.

In discussing this problem, much of Laura's history came out. She explained that she began showing signs of OCD at the age of seven, with her first symptom being hand washing. After a few months, the washing compulsion changed (as it so often does with people who have OCD) to another compulsion—to color in with pencil every letter such as *o* or *p* or *a*. Another particularly time-consuming ritual Laura had to complete was to count to fifty in between reading or writing each word. Because this made her much slower at reading and writing than any of the other children, and because she was unable to finish her tests for the same reason, she was eventually put into a special school with children who had mental retardation. Laura was determined that no one would ever know what her underlying problem was, so she went along with this unfortunate placement.

Laura's father was dead, her mother was busy working two jobs, and her grandmother never seemed to understand what was happening with her granddaughter, so there was no one who could stand up for her. At night, after finishing

her rituals, Laura read her sister's schoolbooks, and in this way, she educated herself. As Laura approached high school age, plans were made to send her to a special high school fifty miles away. Just at that time, the compulsions died down and one of her teachers, who had sometimes commented that Laura was unlike the other students with learning problems, suggested she be put into the local high school. There, she surprised everyone by doing well and even went on to the local junior college, where she met her husband.

Obsessive-compulsive disorder often adds tension to relationships.

Laura now needed help to handle her compulsions so that she could work on her marriage. Anafranil helped by inhibiting her presynaptic neurons from reabsorbing serotonin, and her compulsions started to fade. However, her relationship with her husband still needed work. Behavior therapy was added and is now working slowly.

Drug treatment can help relieve the obsessions and compulsions experi-enced by someone with OCD.

4 | Treatment Description

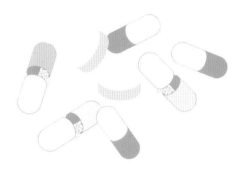

June, summer after junior year

This may be the single weirdest thing that's ever happened to me. I lost my first job today, after just three days, but I have to explain why.

I finished my junior year a week ago, and Mom and Dad said a summer job might be good for me. I applied at the new donut store that just opened by the mall, and they wanted me to work the cash register. I told them no, I'd rather just work in the kitchen, making the donuts. (It seemed like there'd be less chance of having to check my work making donuts. I can't even imagine the checking I'd have to do if I worked the cash register!)

I started on Saturday morning, and Dad dropped me off because he and Mom needed both cars. I was supposed to be there at 7:00 A.M., and I knew it would be hard to make it on time, but I set my alarm clock for 4:00 A.M. so I'd have plenty of time to shower and get dressed. Things went pretty well that first day. It was like so much new stuff was going on that my mind didn't have a chance to make me check things. And the other workers are a lot of fun. There was a lot of laughing and clowning around, because we all felt pretty stupid trying to learn how to make donuts!

On Sunday morning, I had the car to drive myself to work. I got my license in March, and I've driven a lot since then, but almost always with one of my parents in the car. You can tell they don't really trust me yet to drive alone a lot. I think it's because they sometimes see the strange stuff I do at home (although mostly I can hide the checking, and they've given up on trying to get me to shower quicker—they just say I'm a teenager and I'll grow out of it), and even though they're too nice to say it out loud, they secretly think there's some-thing wrong with me. But they probably thought, Hey, it's only a mile to work. What can happen?

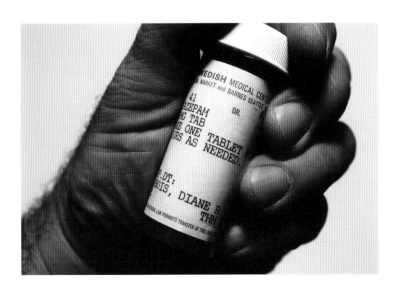

Psychiatric medications are some of the most effective forms of treatment for OCD.

If they only knew. When I drove through our neighborhood, it was still really quiet, and I didn't see a single person. I don't have any idea how to explain what happened next. I was just about two blocks from the donut shop, and all of a sudden, this idea just pops into my head that I might have hit someone on the way to work. It was so strong it made me feel sick to my stomach. I tried to push it away. I mean, how could I have possibly hit somebody when there wasn't even anybody out yet? It was ridiculous.

Then I recognized that gnawing kind of scared feeling in my gut. I knew if I didn't go back and check the feeling would only get worse and worse. I'd never be able to stand it. I checked the car clock. I had fifteen minutes till I had to punch in. I turned the car around and went back over every single block, scanning both sides of the street. Of course there was nothing there. I turned the car around again and headed for the donut shop.

I was only a block away, with just two minutes to spare, when the feeling hit. This time, whatever it is in my head told me that I had probably killed *someone, and their body could have been thrown off the road by the impact—into the bushes, the gutter, somewhere. That's when I started to panic. I knew I had to be at work. I had no time to spare now. But if I didn't go check, the anxiety would kill me. I was already dripping sweat, just from the panic.*

I didn't know what to do. It made me so angry and so scared and sick—all at the same time—that I started crying. But I knew I had to go back.

I found a place to park the car and started to walk both sides of the route I had taken to the donut shop. I searched every gutter and behind every bush and tree. It took me an hour, and when I finally was able to quit checking and go punch in at work, my supervisor met me at the time clock.

"Do you know you're an hour late? Where on earth have you been?" he demanded.

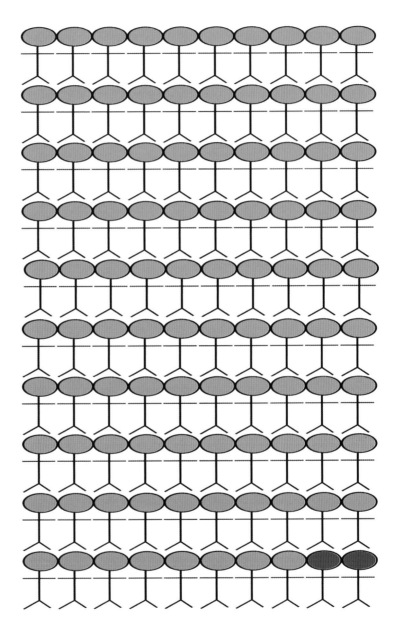

Out of every hundred people, about two will have OCD.

How Many People Have OCD?

In epidemiological studies in the United States, the percentage of people found to be afflicted with OCD is two to three percent of the population. This statistic shows that OCD is more common than schizophrenia. Studies done in Canada, the United Kingdom, Puerto Rico, Germany, Taiwan, Korea, and the Netherlands report a prevalence of 1.9 to 2.5 percent, though some researchers later proposed the percentages be lowered to one to two percent. Among studies of children and adolescents, the prevalence range is two to 3.6 percent.

For a second, I actually thought about telling him the truth—I just felt like I couldn't stand it anymore. Instead, I hung my head and said, "Sorry. I didn't hear my alarm go off."

"You overslept for an hour?" he said, and I could see that look in his eyes, like he was wondering how anybody could be so stupid. But what could I say that wouldn't make it worse?

This morning I left an hour early for work, just in case, and I took a different route. I almost made it, too. Nothing happened on my way and I realized when I got to the parking lot at 7:00 A.M. that if I went in, I'd look stupid in an entirely different way. One day an hour late, the next day an hour early—my supervisor would think I couldn't even tell time! So I pulled back out onto the highway and went for just a short drive, thinking how good it felt to be free and not worrying. That was my mistake.

The same thoughts started up again, even worse than the day before. It was garbage pickup day in the neighborhood where I was driving, and everybody had garbage cans and recycling bins out by the curb. If I'd hit someone with my car—and I was growing surer and surer that I had—they could have dragged themselves to the curb and then fallen behind one of the garbage cans. First I had to get out and check behind every single can and bin. Then, just when I thought I was finished, I had to go back and recheck the route I'd taken the day before. There I was, in my navy blue donut shop uniform, searching the neighborhood for a body—a dead or injured body—which I knew I couldn't have hit. But I had to search. I had no choice.

This time, I was an hour and a half late.

When I punched in at the time clock, the supervisor saw me. "I think we probably won't be requiring your services anymore," he said, and I swear there was ice dripping off his words. I stood there, so ashamed, without any idea what I was supposed to say. How could I explain it to him when I couldn't even explain it to myself?

"You're fired!*" he hollered, angry that I didn't seem to be leaving fast enough. I understood why he was so angry. I guess I would have felt the same way if I'd been him.*

So here I am, just a week into the summer before my senior year, and I already have to explain to my parents why I got fired from my first real job. I have no friends, no job, no life. Looks like I'll have all the time I need to check things—a whole long, boring summer. Maybe even a whole long, boring lifetime, since I'll never be able to go to college or hold down a job. And right now, I don't think I ever even want to drive a car again. I worry sometimes, in the middle of the night, that I'll end up sleeping on a park bench with newspapers over me, like the street people we see when we go into the city. And I can't help wondering if some of them started out like me.

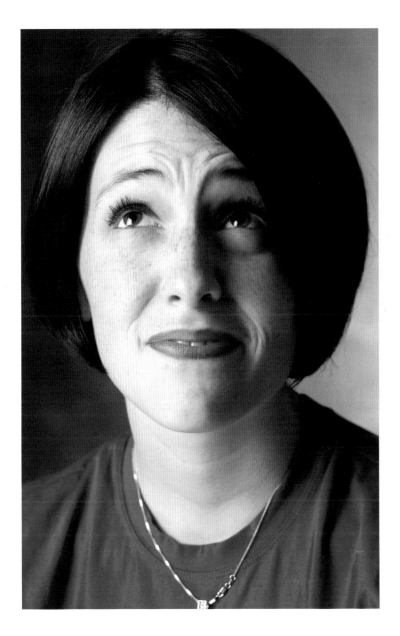

When a person has OCD, her compulsions may land her in uncomfortable or embarrassing situations.

In 1988, an unusual story appeared in the Associated Press. It told of an accidental way in which OCD was cured. The subject, a young man in his twenties named George, became suicidal because of his compulsion to continually wash himself. Intending to kill himself, he put a gun in his mouth and fired. The bullet lodged in the left frontal lobe of his brain, performing a lobotomy. When George recovered, he went on to college and was able to lead a normal life, free of obsessive-compulsive symptoms.

HISTORICAL TREATMENT

Lobotomies

Sal was like Amanda; he struggled with compulsions. Although he had been a trusted worker, family man, and churchgoer, he suddenly developed a compulsion that threatened to bring his life to ruin. His compulsion was hoarding, and he began by picking up small bits of trash on the street or in his home and keeping them. His wife begged him to stop, then threatened to leave him if he didn't, but soon bags and bags full of trash crowded his house and were piled on the furniture.

Sal couldn't stop. His compulsion grew even stronger, and soon he could not resist picking up even tiny pieces of paper. His habit of collecting trash began to take up more and more hours of his day, until he was no longer able to keep his job. Finally, Sal was hospitalized and had an operation that "cured" his compulsion.

This happened in the 1940s, a time when prefrontal *lobotomies* were sometimes used to treat brain disorders. Such procedures are rarely used now, as they involve cutting all connections between the frontal lobe of the brain

GLOSSARY

lobotomies:
Surgical procedures in which the front part of the brain is disconnected from the rest of the brain.

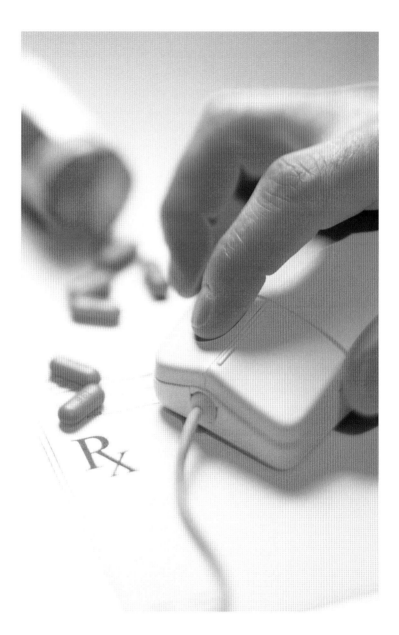

Medical practitioners often prescribe an SSRI for obsessive-compulsive disorder.

gain an important clue to help them understand what causes obsessive-compulsive disorder. Psychiatric drug treatment of OCD has now expanded to include several drugs, mostly SSRIs.

CURRENT PSYCHIATRIC DRUG TREATMENTS FOR OBSESSIVE-COMPULSIVE DISORDER

Serotonin

When Sheila's depression became so severe that she couldn't function anymore, she finally agreed to see a doctor. The doctor prescribed amitriptyline HCl (a TCA), and her depression began to get better. However, there was something she hadn't told the doctor, and she feared it would throw her right back into depression if she didn't deal with it. She just couldn't figure out how to tell her doctor about it because she found it very embarrassing.

Sheila fought a never-ending battle with what she privately called her "strange habits," for lack of a better name. She could never finish cleaning her house, even though she routinely spent twelve to eighteen hours per day working at it. Sheila lived alone, supported by a trust fund from her parents, so no one was aware of how she spent her hours.

How Long Do People Wait to Get Help?

Because of their intense embarrassment, most people are extremely secretive about their OCD symptoms. According to Pato and Zohar, authors of *Current Treatments of Obsessive-Compulsive Disorder,* the usual time reported before people get help is seven years.

Scrubbing the floors with a scrub brush was a daily occurrence for Sheila. She used a toothbrush along the base-
boards and counters as well as around faucets at the sink.
She dusted seven to eight times a day, and she became frantic on sunny days, when she could see dust particles floating
through the air ready to land on the furniture she had just
cleaned.

Sheila also vacuumed several times each day and or-
dered and reordered her kitchen cupboards and dresser
drawers many times throughout the week. There was so
much work to do, and the weight of it felt so heavy to her,
that many nights she wished she could drop off to sleep and
never wake up.

Then Sheila saw a program on television about obsessive-compulsive disorder; she watched while she reorga-
nized the pantry. When the people on TV mentioned excessive cleaning, Sheila stopped, a soup can in each hand, and
listened to the rest of the program. Suddenly, she recog-

*A person with OCD may be obsessed with fears of germs—and
this obsession may compel her to wash her hands over and
over. She may wash so much that her skin becomes raw.*

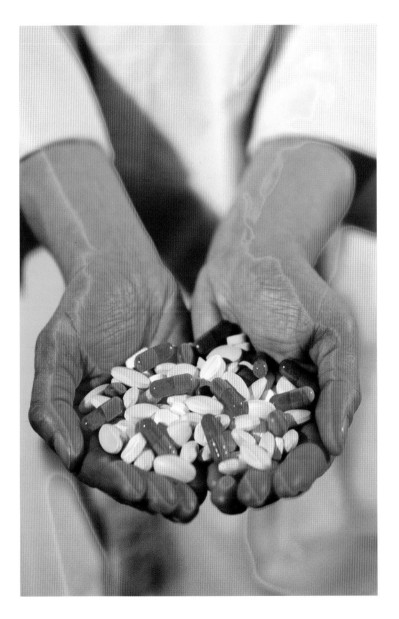

Like many physical diseases, OCD can be treated with medication.

nized her nonstop cleaning for what it was—one of the very symptoms they were discussing. Tears ran down her cheeks as Sheila realized that there were other people like her; that her "strange habits" could be part of a *disease.*

This time, when she went back to her doctor, she told him the whole story, "strange habits" and all. He talked to her at length about her cleaning and explained that, while amitriptyline had helped with the depression, it would have no effect on obsessive-compulsive disorder.

"I'll start you on clomipramine, instead, which is effective for both depression and OCD," he told her. "Try taking it at bedtime each night, because sometimes it makes people feel sleepy."

Sheila began taking 25 milligrams per day, adding another 25 milligrams every third day as her doctor had directed, until she reached 250 milligrams per day. After a few months of this treatment, Sheila was well enough to begin

Medical practitioners prescribe the right dose of drug for each patient.

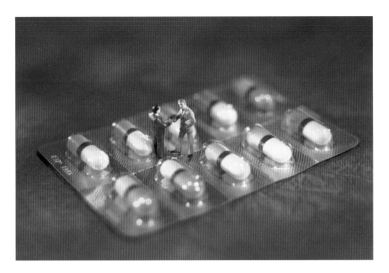

Used appropriately, medication can contribute to physical health and emotional well-being.

taking accounting classes at the local junior college. After her strange habits disappeared, she remained on a low maintenance dose of clomipramine, and eventually took a part-time job in accounting.

Fluoxetine

When they had their first child, Daniel and Joanna struck an agreement—she would continue her job as a highly paid trial lawyer while he stayed home full time with baby Chloe. All went well for the first few days of their new arrangement.

Then Daniel began noticing strange thoughts flitting through his mind, thoughts of doing terrible harm to Chloe. He was devastated that he could even think such things about this baby he loved so dearly. He had always struggled with being what his parents had termed a "nervous person," and he had had facial *tics* during much of his childhood

GLOSSARY

tics: *Involuntary, sudden, and recurrent movements or vocalizations.*

Facial tics are sudden, spasmodic movements.

and adolescence. These had faded as he grew up, however, so Daniel was totally unprepared for the experience of these horrible thoughts. Worse, he was afraid to tell anyone, for fear they might take Chloe away from him. He knew with absolute certainty he would never act on any of these disturbing thoughts, but what if a doctor wouldn't believe him?

Daniel began to have trouble sleeping, and he lost weight for the next several months. Finally, haunted by the continuing thoughts, he hired a sitter for Chloe and spent a day at the library of a nearby university, researching both on-line and in print. To his relief, he found that his problem was not unusual; such thoughts were often a symptom of OCD. He copied several articles on obsessive-compulsive disorder and scheduled an appointment with his family doctor, taking the articles along to show him.

Daniel was put on fluoxetine, at a dose of 40 milligrams per day, which was gradually increased to 80 milligrams per

When someone has OCD, he may be ashamed to admit his symptoms.

day. After several months, the frightening thoughts had faded to the point where Daniel could comfortably ignore the remaining few that raced through his mind just a few times per month.

Fluvoxamine and Sertraline

When Angela was put on fluvoxamine, her parents and doctor had great hope that she would finally be able to stop being preoccupied with her fear of contamination from chemical poisons. She constantly checked the house, a room at a time, for any suspicious damp spots on the floors or carpets—anything that might indicate an intruder had spilled deadly chemicals there to sabotage her family. She got up several times each night to check, turning on all the lights and doing a painstaking inspection, frantic that her whole family might inhale some toxic substance and be killed in their sleep.

Fluvoxamine, however, made Angela so nauseous that she couldn't tolerate it, even when the doctor lowered her dose. The doctor then switched her to sertraline, a drug she tolerated much better. Sertraline has been found to frequently be effective at the low dose of 50 milligrams, as it was in Angela's case. Within four months of taking sertraline, combined with psychotherapy, Angela was able to sleep through the night and was able to stop checking the floors of her house almost completely.

Paroxetine

When Brady was ten, he suddenly started having trouble in school. Always a good student, he began to feel driven to do more and more, and to do it better. He became very upset when he was unable to finish a test or assignment. At home, he was so preoccupied with cleaning his room that he no longer went outside to play with neighbor-

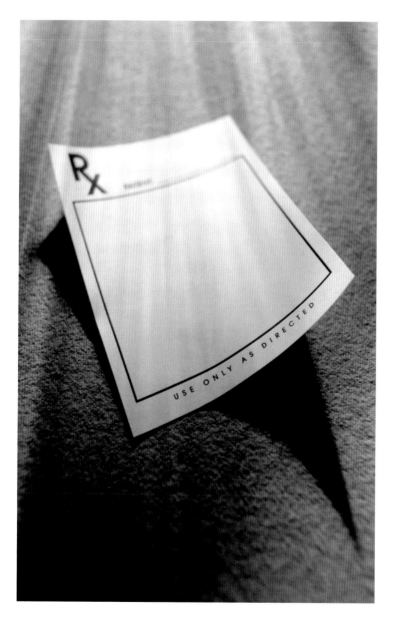

Successful drug therapy depends on following exactly your medical practitioner's directions.

hood friends. He cleaned the room every day, making sure every pen and pencil on his desk were lined up perfectly and that even the smallest wrinkle was smoothed out of his comforter. Finally, Brady became so frantic about the least bit of disorder in his room that he entered it only to get clean clothes from the dresser and closet. At night, he slept in his sleeping bag in front of his bedroom door rather than go inside and "mess it up" again.

Brady's parents took him to a psychiatric clinic for evaluation and treatment. There, he had a complete physical examination, including blood tests to check his **blood count** and a **urinalysis**. Afterward, Brady was put on Paxil. Within the first several weeks, Brady began to pay no attention to his homework at all and wanted only to play. The doctor adjusted his medication, giving him a smaller amount of Paxil. Within a few more weeks, Brady was able to enjoy his room

GLOSSARY

blood count: The ratio of different types of cells in a specified amount of blood.

urinalysis: A chemical analysis of the urine.

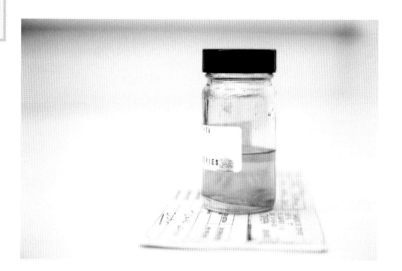

Before starting a psychiatric medication, a complete physical exam is recommended. This may include a urine test.

again (including sleeping in his own bed) and to make decisions comfortably about when to study and when to play.

As we can see from these stories, drug therapy offers real hope to people with OCD. The chemicals in psychiatric drugs work with the body's own chemicals. They help the body to function normally, allowing patients to live more normal lives.

Psychiatric drugs are made from chemicals that affect the action of other chemicals inside the human brain.

5 | Case Studies

October, senior year

I don't even know how to describe what happened at school today. I'm not sure I have the words.

They told us last week that our school had been chosen to participate in a research project by some big important hospital in Boston. It was called an epidemiological survey, *and we were all supposed to be interviewed by these doctors as part of their study of some disease I'd never heard of before. If you didn't want to be involved, you had to bring a note signed by a parent, and then you could be excused.*

I was so busy checking homework last night that I forgot to give my parents the note, so I had to be interviewed. I mean, I could've called my mom and still gotten out of it, but I figured I'd just stay quiet, not say too much, and they'd never have a clue. Whatever's been going on in my brain these last few years, it's taught me one thing for sure—to be a good actor. Most people just think I'm really snobby, because I almost never talk to anybody at school. And they all think I'm pretty slow, mentally, because I take so long to do everything. But it puzzles them that I still get good grades—the two things just don't seem to go together.

Anyway, it came my turn to go into the school nurse's office, where they were doing their interviews. The woman who talked to me introduced herself as Dr. Baxter, and after a few minutes of talk about school, she started to ask me some questions. At first it was just the usual—height, weight, age, place of birth, stuff like that. Then she looked me in the eye and asked me if I had any habits like washing my hands over and over.

"No," I answered.

"How about counting?"

"What do you mean?" I asked.

Dr. Baxter explained that some people feel the need to count objects over and over, for no particular reason; that others have to count to a certain number—say, fifty—before certain activities or have to do things either an even or an odd amount of times. Stuff like that.

I shook my head. "I don't do that," I said. But without consciously meaning to, I put a little emphasis on the word "that." Dr. Baxter looked up instantly.

"Do you find yourself doing something similar?" she asked.

I hesitated. There was no way I could let her know what was really going on—I'd die of embarrassment if she found out. But I sensed she might know something. Maybe, if I phrased my question the right way, I could get some information out of her.

I decided to go with the easy one first. "Well, sometimes I have a little trouble figuring out if my bedroom door is really locked at night." I immediately felt my face flush and laughed

Admitting you have a problem is often a necessary step toward finding the right answers for your situation.

a little to try to cover up my embarrassment. "Sounds crazy, doesn't it?"

Dr. Baxter didn't laugh at all. She just said, "Not to me, Amanda. I've known some very intelligent and creative people who were 'door-checkers.' Tell me, does your door checking interfere with your life in any way?"

Not the door checking, I thought. That's simple compared to the other stuff. Ask me about the other stuff! I couldn't bring myself to say it first. "Not really," I answered her question at last.

"Are there other habits that do interfere?" she asked.

I shrugged my shoulders. "Maybe one, two. Nothing big." I winced inside as I heard myself lie. But I didn't even know what words to use to tell her. I was sitting there gripping the

Checking and rechecking a locked door is a common OCD compulsion.

edge of my seat, wishing she would help me more, and it was like she read my mind.

"May I suggest a few other things that may be bothering you?" Dr. Baxter asked.

I didn't know what else to do, so I nodded.

She mentioned lots of weird stuff, like washing your hands over and over with Mr. Clean or some other household cleaner; or getting pornographic pictures in your mind over and over every day; or saying a prayer over hundreds of times every day to ward off "harm." Then she said "or checking your homework over and over," and I sat up straighter in my chair, though I couldn't bring myself to answer her.

But when she said, "Do you ever have thoughts of hurting anyone? Or that you may have hurt someone? Perhaps with a car you were driving?" I totally embarrassed myself by bursting into tears like a two-year-old.

The doctor didn't seem disgusted, though. She let me cry for a long time, just handing me tissues and smiling encouragingly at me every now and then. At last, when I settled down, she asked, "Would you like to tell me about it, Amanda?"

I told her about everything then—the endless checking that kept me from being able to have a normal life, about losing my job at the donut shop and why, and about how I'd never been able to breathe a word of this to anyone. "And I'm really embarrassed that I'm sitting here bawling my eyes out to a total stranger," I ended, but she just gave me another kind smile and said that a lot of people cry when they first find out they're not the only ones who have all this strange stuff going on inside.

"You mean there are other people like me?" I asked, and when she told me that they estimated there were about six million in the United States alone, I felt as though a big weight slid off my shoulders. I wasn't the strangest person in the uni-

Sometimes the onset of OCD or OCD-like symptoms is connected with a particular event. The most famous of these situations may be seen in Shakespeare's play *Macbeth*. After the king is murdered, Lady Macbeth keeps trying to wash away an imaginary spot on her hands that symbolizes guilt. Today, some people wash their hands excessively in an attempt to "cleanse" their hands from various acts.

verse! Other people had this same thing! I was so excited I could hardly even listen to what she was saying when she first started to tell me about a disease called OCD, which stands for obsessive-compulsive disorder. But as she went on describing it, I got more and more interested. It felt as though someone who had never met me was describing my most private inner thoughts and feelings. Somebody understood. That may be the best gift I've ever been given.

Many people who suffer from OCD feel as though the world opens up for them when they discover that millions of others have the same or similar symptoms and that there is help. In her book *The Boy Who Couldn't Stop Washing*, Dr. Judith Rapoport tells the sad, yet heartwarming story of an OCD sufferer named Robert, an attractive, forty-five-year-old, unmarried physicist. Robert's earliest memory in life was of a compulsion to hold his breath, experienced when he was only two years old and still being pushed in a stroller by his mother. He also remembered being extremely distressed by the fact that although he didn't want to do this terribly unpleasant thing, he knew he *had* to do it.

One compulsion after another appeared in his life, dogging his footsteps, taking up his time, even embarrassing and the brain's deeper parts. Sadly, though Sal's compulsions were decreased dramatically by the lobotomy, he never again left the hospital because the procedure also left him socially disabled. As sometimes happened with other people who endured this procedure, Sal began behaving in inappropriate ways, such as pinching young women or urinating in the street. This early experimental "treatment" for OCD left Sal in a sad condition.

Drug Therapy

In the 1970s, when Dr. Rapoport and the NIMH began their study of adolescents with OCD, they discovered that Anafranil was very effective in both adolescents and adults. One question that arose was why the widely used antidepressant, Tofranil, which is similar in chemical structure to Anafranil, was not also effective in treating OCD. Researchers realized that the small difference in formula between the two drugs must be the cause of Anafranil's ability to blunt or remove obsessions and compulsions in OCD patients. If researchers understood this difference, they would

---

Off-Label Prescriptions

The FDA bases its approval on specific research results. Sometimes, a particular use for a drug may have been thoroughly researched by many studies, while other uses lack the same amount of research. In that case, the drug label will only include the uses that have met the FDA's stringent research requirements. Physicians, however, may continue to prescribe that drug for other "off-label" uses.

A person with OCD may be compelled to hold his breath until his face turns red and he is forced to take a breath.

him in public. In Catholic school, he felt forced by his compulsions to memorize religious passages and stories of the lives of saints. At night he had to read and reread the same pages again and again until he could repeat every word exactly.

In high school he was humiliated by his compulsion to check the zipper of his pants over and over, an action that resulted in the other boys making jokes about him and the girls avoiding him. Robert felt that the ten years this compulsion lasted were possibly the loneliest time of his entire life.

Robert had a compulsion to check his zipper again and again.

In graduate school, he fell in love with another graduate student, who returned his affection. Their relationship lasted for several years, but Robert was sure he could never let her know what was going on inside his head. Trivial rituals were still eating up his days. One ritual, for example, meant that he must recall every single guest on the TV talk show he'd watched the previous night before he could go on with his day. If he couldn't remember every talk show guest, he had to look it up in the paper or even call the station.

When he was occupied with this and other rituals, the girl he loved thought he was either angry or bored. At last, Robert and the girl split up and went their separate ways. Robert became professionally successful by building a one-man consulting firm, a job that gave him both the time and the privacy to carry out his compulsive rituals. It was also a job that was very lonely.

Even though this intelligent and sensitive man had worked with a wonderful therapist for over a thousand hours to combat his disorder, he was still locked in his OCD prison. Other people were pushed out of his life by his need for privacy to perform the endless, meaningless rituals that took up his days.

After years of determining every day that he would beat his compulsions and just as many years of failing, Robert finally decided he must not have the character and discipline to combat whatever it was that was wrong with him. Then he saw a TV program, *20/20*, about people with obsessive-compulsive disorder in which Dr. Judith L. Rapoport was referenced. He got in touch with Dr. Rapoport and her staff and started on Anafranil. After seeing the *20/20* program, Robert had begun keeping a record of his compulsions, recording how many thoughts and rituals were happening per hour. Soon after he started on Anafranil, the number of

compulsions decreased—and those that remained lost their power to control his life.

Not every person who begins using Anafranil is helped by the medication. Of those who are, however, not all see their compulsions and obsessions cease. In some people, the compulsions and obsessions simply begin to lose their feeling of irresistibility, and the patient finds he or she can refuse the thought. In others, the thoughts come briefly, and then fade away on their own.

Usually, people need a number of weeks or months before they see the full effect of the medication prescribed for them. In Robert's case, six months after he began taking Anafranil, he saw such improvement that he began to believe he might be able to live a fairly normal life. In a storybook kind of ending, he searched for the girl he had loved in graduate school and found that, not only had she never married but she had never stopped thinking about him. They were reunited and began planning for a future together.

Over and over, people with OCD talk about the need to keep their rituals secret from everyone in their lives, even husbands, wives, children, and other loved ones, just as Robert did. The reason most commonly given is fear that people will believe them to be crazy, since those with obsessive-compulsive disorder often fear this to be the case. Spouses of people with OCD often recount feeling that their spouse is bored or angry with them, and they spend a great deal of time trying to find out what they have done to provoke these feelings. Frustration usually results, and many times relationships break down under the strain of total secrecy on the part of the person with OCD. OCD sufferers are nearly twice as likely than others to never marry; if married, they are more likely to get divorced.

Compulsions may get in the way of relationships.

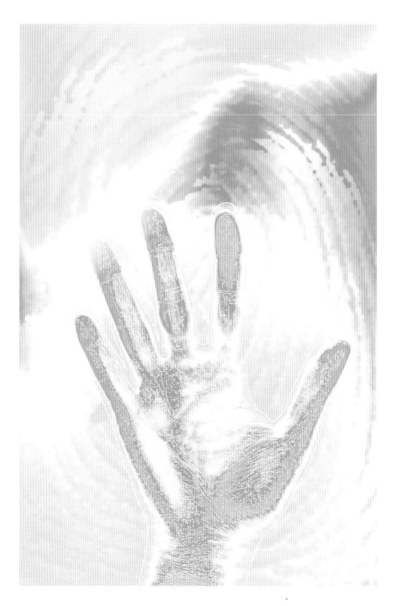

A person with OCD may feel trapped by her obsessions and compulsions.

AIDS AND OCD

In the 1980s, AIDS (acquired immunodeficiency syndrome) became a part of the world's vocabulary. For a large percentage of people with obsessive-compulsive disorder, avoiding AIDS became yet one more obsession—even if they understood how the disease was transmitted and knew they had never actually been exposed.

Annaliese was an operating room nurse who more than ten years ago had been accidentally poked by a needle that had a patient's blood on it. The patient was not **HIV positive**, and over the last decade Annaliese has been tested and retested for HIV. Every test came back negative. Even though Annaliese understood the biology involved, she remained irrationally convinced that she could have contracted AIDS through this incident. She talked her doctor into ordering nearly every AIDS test available, including having her blood cultured. When the results came back negative, she was convinced the lab had made a mistake in its procedures, or had confused her records with those of another patient. She washed her hands scores of times each day, for several minutes each time. Eventually, she had to leave her job because she could no longer carry out her duties as a nurse and still fulfill her compulsions to wash her hands and to repeatedly have every AIDS test available.

As a single mother, Annaliese had a will made out leaving everything to her children; convinced she will be leaving them motherless, she has named her own mother and father as their legal guardians. Her obsessions and compulsions are controlling her life.

GLOSSARY

HIV positive: Having the human immunodeficiency virus, which can cause AIDS.

Religious obsessions are common among people with OCD.

Behavioral Psychotherapy for Religious Obsessions

Ignatius of Loyola (1548) formulated a way to improve the soul, based on the principle of *agere contra* (do the opposite). In 1973, a Catholic priest named O'Flaherty wrote about a treatment plan based on Loyola's work. In this plan, patients with obsessive-compulsive disorder are advised to take the following four steps:

- Book the incidents.
  Patients keep a diary of every event that precipitates a need to carry out rituals.
- Systematically study the incidents.
  This is a form of behavioral analysis in which therapists and patients note the people, places, and events that give rise to the incidents.
- Reject by distraction.
  Patients are taught to focus their minds on a neutral subject instead of thinking about whether they have sinned.
- Break the habits.
  If patients find themselves preoccupied with obsessive thoughts or carrying out rituals, they should lay their hands on their hearts and grieve that they have fallen.

Adapted from *Current Treatments of Obsessive-Compulsive Disorder*, by Pato and Zohar, p. 184.

SCRUPULOSITY

The summer before she began eighth grade, Becky attended a special weekend youth convention sponsored by several Catholic groups in her state. It was a meeting of several hundred teens, filled with singing and small prayer groups. The weekend was a joyful time for her, except for the mention of Satan in one sermon. For some reason, the word Satan filled her with a sense of dread.

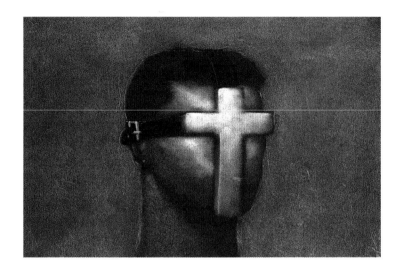

Faith can be a constructive force in a person's life—but religion can also fuel various forms of psychiatric disorders.

When she returned home, she suddenly began having thoughts about physically hurting her baby sister—something she knew she would never actually do, but the thoughts alone caused her great guilt and pain. Becky was convinced Satan was putting these thoughts into her head. She felt that the only way to combat them was to pray. Every time one of these thoughts popped into her head, she had to stop whatever she was doing and pray for half an hour. This worked out during the summer vacation, but when school started up again, Becky found she couldn't keep up with her eighth-grade classes; she had to continually stop listening to the teacher and pray silently at her desk. Unable to stop the thoughts on her own, Becky began going to confession several times a week. Soon her entire life revolved around these rituals.

At home, Becky faced increasing conflict with her parents. Convinced that she was an evil person who needed to stay away from the baby sister she had formerly doted on, Becky spent hours alone in her room. Her parents had no idea what was really going on in Becky's mind or that she was spending most of those hours in prayer. From her apparent lack of interest in her sister and the rest of the family, they concluded she was simply becoming a "self-centered" teenager. Becky didn't try to convince them differently. *What would I say?* she thought. *They'd just think I was crazy if I told them what was really going on.*

After several months, her eighth-grade teachers alerted the principal that Becky, who had once been an honor role student, was now in danger of failing most of her classes. The principal contacted Becky's parents, and a meeting that included the school psychologist was called. When confronted with the possibility of failing her classes, Becky insisted that this was a punishment she deserved. Although they questioned her closely as to what she had done that was deserving of punishment, Becky refused to say.

About thirty minutes into the meeting, Becky suddenly experienced one of the frightening thoughts about hurting her sister again. She immediately tuned out all the people in the room; although they didn't realize what she was doing, she began to pray silently. After several frustrating minutes of trying to get Becky to respond, her parents and the principal gave up.

The psychologist, who had some experience with obsessive-compulsive behaviors, began to suspect that Becky might have problems with OCD. She asked for a private meeting with the girl. When they met, Becky at first refused to explain why she had not responded to the adults at the principal's meeting. The psychologist, however, remained warm and understanding. Finally, Becky began to feel comfortable enough to make an attempt to explain.

"I couldn't talk to any of you just then," she began.

"You could hear us, though?" the psychologist probed.

"Of course I could hear you. I just couldn't answer because my sister could have died if I had quit praying right then," Becky said, as though she were giving a perfectly logical explanation. Seeing the psychologist's puzzled look, she added, "I have to stop everything and pray every time I have the bad thoughts. If I don't, the baby could die. It would be my punishment."

Once Becky got that much of the story out, the rest followed quickly. By this time, Becky was praying for three to four hours every day; she told her parents she was going to the library after school to study, but in reality she was going to confession. Repeated prayer and confession gave her a fleeting sense that she would not be punished, but that con-

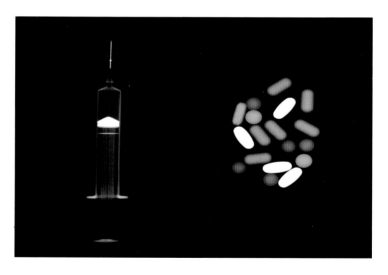

Psychiatric drugs offer the hope for a cure to people with OCD.

fidence passed quickly, leaving her with the overwhelming feeling that she must do it all again, over and over.

When Becky began therapy, she was given Luvox, which helped reduce her compulsions in a matter of three weeks. Along with that, however, her parents, who had been meeting with their priest and doing a great deal of reading on this subject for themselves, felt that Becky needed to understand the idea of ***scrupulosity.*** This is the Catholic Church's name for a recognized form of obsessive-compulsive disorder.

The Christian church, both Protestant and Catholic, has long recognized that religion is a primary area for obsessions and compulsions to occur. Ignatius of Loyola and Martin Luther, religious leaders from the sixteenth century, exhibited symptoms of OCD.

Throughout history, real-life people have suffered from the strange malady we know today as obsessive-compulsive disorder. Thankfully, people with this disorder now have reason to hope for a cure. Psychiatric drugs can help them combat their disease.

No one should put total faith in psychiatric medication. These drugs also have risks and side effects that must be carefully monitored.

6 | Risks and Side Effects

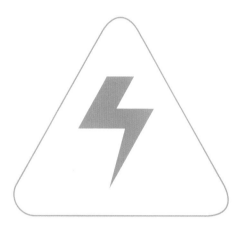

*O*ctober, senior year

I had another meeting with Dr. Baxter today, only this time her whole team was included. They all acted like I was a very important "find," which made me feel good. They asked me questions and listened to my answers most of the morning, and several of them were taking notes; then they thanked me for my time and said my information would help them treat other people with OCD.

When I was alone with Dr. Baxter again, she asked me if I wanted to try one of the medicines they have now for OCD. I knew right away I had to try anything that might help me get rid of this disease.

"Yes, I really do," I told her. "But first, I need to ask you something. Would you talk to my parents and my sister with me? And explain everything you've told me? They're never go-ing to believe this if it just comes from me."

She smiled and nodded. "I'll be glad to, Amanda. In fact, if you really want to pursue using medication for this, I'll have to get your parents' permission. And they'll have to come with you to the clinic first so we can get a firm diagnosis and run some tests."

That evening, I went back to the school to meet with Dr. Baxter again. Only this time, Mom and Dad were with me. I didn't really tell them much about what was going on, because I wanted to let Dr. Baxter do it. I was afraid I'd mess up everything if I tried to tell them about OCD by myself.

Dr. Baxter and I had agreed that I would talk first, telling my parents about the checking. Then I told them the real reason I lost my job at the donut shop. I'd been so humiliated

Admitting you have a problem is often difficult.

Family support can play an important role in treating OCD.

about what happened that it hadn't even mattered to me what I told them. After all, I couldn't possibly tell them the truth, so I had just told them that I'd quit. There was a lot of arguing afterward, and Dad especially had acted like he was totally disgusted with me. He'd been on me all summer about why I wouldn't go get another job.

I'll never forget how their faces looked that night when they heard the real reason. Then Dr. Baxter stepped in and explained about OCD. Mom had been crying a little ever since I had described just how bad the checking had become, but when I told about why I got fired, Dad broke down and put his head in his hands, his shoulders shaking. Then they both came and put their arms around me and we cried together for a while.

"Why didn't you ever tell us?" Dad kept saying. "What made you keep it all inside this way? We could have been helping you all this time."

I explained how weird I'd felt, as though I was the only person in the world with such a strange problem. How I was so ashamed to let anybody know how awful my private world had become.

The following week we went to Dr. Baxter's clinic in Boston, about three hours away from our house. There she did a lot of tests and had the lab draw blood. She also talked to my parents and me again for several hours, sometimes together and sometimes privately. At the end of the time, she confirmed what we already knew—I was a definite yes for obsessive-compulsive disorder. Then she sent me home with enough Anafranil (clomipramine) for two weeks, explaining carefully how I was supposed to take the medicine, starting out with a small dose and gradually working up to a bigger one. She told my parents and me about side effects to watch out for and had them make another appointment for me for two weeks from then. I can't wait to see if this works!

Serotonin Syndrome

When there is more serotonin than needed in parts of the brain, patients may experience confusion, slurred speech, diaphoresis, nausea, diarrhea, abdominal cramps, hyper-reflexia (increased action of the reflexes), insomnia, problems with blood coagulation, and flushing. Excessive serotonin can be a result of taking more than one psychiatric drug at a time, or combining them in the wrong way. Serotonin syndrome can lead to seizures or death. However, it is a rare condition.

November 30

Well, it didn't work so well. I mean, the medicine was starting to help with the checking just a little, but I couldn't handle the dizziness and the tremors. I also had a lot of nausea. After a couple of weeks, I was so discouraged I was ready to give up. We called Dr. Baxter and she switched me to Luxor (fluvox-amine) last week. The nausea's gone, and so are the tremors and dizziness. But I'm still checking and doing all the other OCD stuff. I'm beginning to doubt if there's anything that will really help me.

Like Amanda, patients sometimes become discouraged by the side effects of the drugs prescribed for them. Side effects are caused for the most part when drugs affect neurotransmitters and receptors that are not involved in any way in the illness at question. But because there are now so many drugs available for treating OCD, patients have more

treatment options than ever before; they should work with their doctors to find the right medication for them.

WHAT IS A SIDE EFFECT?

Jack Gorman, M.D., in his book *The New Psychiatry*, gives a simple summary of what a drug side effect is: "A side effect is anything a drug does that we don't want it to do." He goes on to explain that any chemical substance we put into our bodies will affect more than just the one part of our body that we want it to affect. He likens this to the food we eat, using a steak as an example of good taste and a good source of needed protein for our bodies. He then points out that steak can do other things to our bodies, however, including

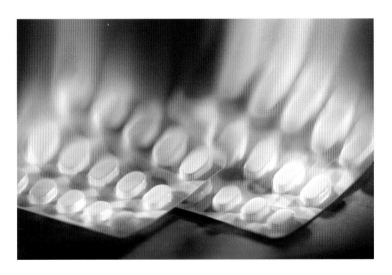

Many drugs produce unwanted side effects that must be balanced with that medication's benefits.

increasing our cholesterol level and adding unwanted weight. Some people will consider both the positive and negative effects of eating steak and decide to go ahead and eat the steak, because the benefits outweigh the risks.

Common side effects for SSRIs:

- fatigue
- agitation (occasionally)
- decreased sexual drive/impaired sexual response

Side effects for TCAs may include:

- weight gain
- dry mouth
- constipation
- sweating
- light-headedness due to low blood pressure

Drugs can provide needed benefits, but they also produce unwanted side effects (though some may be much more serious than the "side effects" of eating steak). In some cases, the benefits will outweigh the side effects to the degree that many people suffering from obsessive-compulsive disorder will decide they will take the drugs and find ways to deal with the side effects.

A combination of therapies often offers real hope to someone who suffers from OCD.

7 | Alternative and Supplementary Treatments

*J*anuary, senior year

Guess what? I wrote once before that I thought the old Amanda was gone forever, but I was wrong! I think I found a little bit of my old self again, and every day now, things are changing for the better.

At first, nothing happened when I started taking the Luvox. I couldn't help thinking that, given how things have been for me since eighth grade, Luvox would probably work for every other OCD patient but me. But after a couple of weeks, I noticed I didn't feel like I had to go through the entire shower ritual. The thoughts of doing it were still there, sure, but I didn't have *to do all those stupid steps. So I didn't.*

By the end of the first two weeks, I was only checking my math problems once after I finished—the way a normal person would; the way I used to. We went back to Boston to the clinic at that point, and Dr. Baxter asked me a lot of questions and took notes again. When I told her about the good changes, she got this huge smile on her face.

She asked me about side effects, so I told her I was sort of constipated and my mouth gets dry sometimes, but that's nothing compared to the side effects from the first drug. I'm also a little more tired than I think I should be (it's hard to tell if I'm unusually tired, though, since I've been tired for years anyway from staying up checking my homework and getting up so early to shower). She said that all of those things are probably side effects of the medicine. We talked about adding more fiber to my diet and sucking on sugarless candies and some other ways to deal with the side effects.

Anyway, the side effects are worth the chance to have my life back. I can't even begin to describe what a difference it's made at home. My parents are so excited to have me "back," as they put it, they can hardly stand it. And we took Nikki to a special meeting for parents and siblings of people with OCD. She didn't say much at first, but I notice she's more patient now about things like waiting for the shower. Because even though the Luvox has helped a lot, I still have some mild symptoms, so it still takes me a little longer than other people in the shower. Dr. Baxter hopes the symptoms will go away completely after I've been on the drug longer. We'll see.

One of the best things Dr. Baxter is doing is putting people who have similar OCD symptoms in touch with each other. There's this guy named Gene, in a town about an hour from here, who has been going through a lot of the same things as me, except his main problem is getting through doorways! I know that sounds funny, but we've been talking on the phone nearly every day, and he explained that ever since he was about twelve he has to go through this long, involved ritual before he can walk through a doorway. Once it took him two hours to go through his front door when he got home from school, and he says he has to get up an hour early to walk

Finding out you are not alone is a wonderful feeling. Support groups offer people a chance to talk with others like themselves.

through his bedroom and bathroom doorways! I know it sounds like an awful thing to laugh at, but we're not laughing at each other—we're laughing together at this ridiculous disease. Gene's on the honor role at his school, too, and he's been on Luvox for about four months now. He says that when we get together next week, he's so much better that I'll hardly even notice—unless the restaurant where we're going has too many doorways. We both had a good laugh over that. And I told him that I'd do my best to be on time, as long as I didn't have to go back too many times to check the interstate and make sure I hadn't run over anyone. I can actually drive again!

Last week, I asked my parents to go back to the donut shop with me. Together, we sat down and explained to my old boss about OCD. At first he looked at me kind of funny, as though I was making this all up. But after we talked for a

Books can play a role in recovery from OCD. Educating yourself about your disorder is an important step to take!

Obsessive-Compulsive Disorder Self-Test

Here is a list of questions people may ask themselves to determine if they have problems with obsessive-compulsive disorder.

Do you experience unwanted ideas, impulses, or images in your mind?

Do you worry a great deal about getting dirty or about coming into contact with germs or chemicals?

Do you worry that you forgot to lock a door or turn off the stove? Do you have to keep checking over and over to make sure you did these or other activities?

Do you wash your hands repeatedly, many times a day? Do you repeatedly wash objects belonging to you?

Are there actions you must repeat or thoughts you must think over and over in order to feel comfortable?

Positive responses to the above questions may help you decide to talk with your health care professional about the nature of troubling thoughts or impulses you experience.

Adapted from the Anxiety Disorders Association of America, www.adaa.org

---

while, his attitude seemed to change. At the end of our meeting, he said he didn't have any openings right then but that he'd be sure to call me when he did. Now I just need to get up the courage to call Emma. Even if she doesn't understand, there are a lot of people who will.

I'm really grateful for Luvox, but Dr. Baxter says that there are some other kinds of therapy that might help me, too. I'm so excited about having my life back that I'll try whatever she suggests.

BEHAVIORAL TREATMENT

The psychiatric drugs listed in the preceding chapters are the only medications currently known to effectively treat OCD. There are no herbs or other alternative substances known to work on OCD. But behavioral treatments are sometimes effective, both on their own and in combination with drug treatment.

Exposure and blocking procedures often help patients with OCD in the area of rituals. Exposure requires people with OCD to directly confront the ideas or situations they find fear producing. This may or may not be accompanied by imaginary exposure to the feared outcome. Blocking, or response prevention, may help end ritualistic behaviors. The blocking of mental compulsions may require thought stopping or distraction strategies.

Combining exposure and blocking as a treatment for OCD was first done by Meyer in 1966. His patients, who had washing and cleaning rituals, were required to repeatedly

---

Unlock Brain Lock

In Jeffrey M. Schwartz's book, *Brain Lock,* he explains the following four-step system for readers who suffer from OCD:

1. RELABEL. Recognize that obsessive thoughts and urges are the result of OCD.
2. REATTRIBUTE. Realize the intensity of the urge is caused by OCD and is most likely related to a biochemical imbalance in the brain.
3. REFOCUS. Focus your attention on something else, even if only for a few minutes.
4. REVALUE. Refuse to value the OCD thought as significant.

Family understanding helps people with OCD learn to cope with life more effectively.

touch objects that caused them anxiety about contamination and gave them the urge to wash. Other studies show that relaxation training had no effect, but people treated by a licensed practitioner with exposure and response prevention achieved fairly high rates of success in eliminating some OCD behaviors.

THE IMPORTANCE OF FAMILIES

Family support and understanding can make a tremendous difference in lives of people with OCD. Instead of feeling as though they are cut off from family members and must hide their rituals out of shame, people with supportive families can learn to cope in an atmosphere of acceptance and love.

"Guidelines for Living with OCD," described in a pamphlet by Van Noppen and colleagues called *Learning to Live with OCD*, provides helpful points for families who have a member with OCD. Some of these guidelines are included below:

- Learn to recognize the signals that indicate a person is having problems.
- Modify expectations during stressful times.
- Measure progress according to the person's level of functioning.
- Don't make day-to-day comparisons.
- Give recognition for "small" improvements.
- Create a strong, supportive home environment.
- Keep communication clear and simple.
- Set limits, yet be sensitive to the person's mood.
- Keep your family routine "normal."
- Use humor.
- Support the person's medication *regimen*.
- Be flexible.

> **GLOSSARY**
>
> ***regimen:*** *A regular course of action; a systematic plan.*

Obsessive-compulsive disorder is one of the most unusual and challenging disorders faced by the medical profession. The discovery of effective drug treatments is a first step in finding a way to help people with OCD, and as research continues, more medications will be found and approved for use. For now, understanding, acceptance, and appropriate treatment are helping many people with OCD live productive, fulfilled lives.

FURTHER READING

Colas, Emily. *Just Checking, Scenes from the Life of an Obsessive-Compulsive*. New York: Pocket Books, 1998.

Drummond, Edward. *The Complete Guide to Psychiatric Drugs.* New York: John Wiley, 2000.

Gorman, Jack M. *The New Psychiatry.* New York: St. Martin's, 1996.

Gorman, Jack M. *The Essential Guide to Psychiatric Drugs.* New York: St. Martin's Griffin, 1997.

Osborn, Ian. *Tormenting Thoughts and Secret Rituals: The Hidden Epidemic of Obsessive Compulsive Disorder.* New York: Delacorte, 1999.

Pato, Michele Tortora, and Joseph, Zohar *Current Treatments of Obsessive-Compulsive Disorder,* Second Edition. Washington, D.C.: American Psychiatric Publishing, 2001.

Rapoport, Judith L. *The Boy Who Wouldn't Stop Washing; The Experience and Treatment of Obsessive-Compulsive Disorder.* New York: E. P. Dutton, 1989.

FOR MORE INFORMATION

American Psychiatric Association
1400 K St., N.W.
Washington, DC 20005
www.psych.org

American Psychological Association
750 First Street, N.E.
Washington, DC 20002
www.apa.org

Obsessive-Compulsive Foundation
www.ocfoundation.org

OCD Screening Quiz
psychcentral.com/ocdquiz.htm

Publisher's Note:

The Web sites listed on this page were active at the time of publication. The publisher is not responsible for Web sites that have changed their address or discontinued operation since the date of publication. The publisher will review and update the Web sites upon each reprint.

INDEX

BIOGRAPHIES

Shirley Brinkerhoff is a writer, editor, speaker, and musician. She graduated Summa Cum Laude from Cornerstone University with a Bachelor of Music degree, and from Western Michigan University with a Master of Music degree. She has published six young adult novels, seven informational books for young people, scores of short stories and articles, and teaches at writers' conferences throughout the United States.

Mary Ann Johnson is a licensed child and adolescent clinical nurse specialist and a family psychiatric nurse practitioner in the state of Massachusetts. She completed her psychotherapy training at Cambridge Hospital and her psychopharmacology training at Massachusetts General Hospital. She is the director of clinical trials in the pediatric psychopharmacology research unit at Massachusetts General Hospital.

Donald Esherick has spent seventeen years working in the pharmaceutical industry and is currently an associate director of Worldwide Regulatory Affairs with Wyeth Research in Philadelphia, Pennsylvania. He specializes in the chemistry section (manufacture and testing) of investigational and marketed drugs.